BUSH AND BACKWOODS

Bush and Backwoods

A COMPARISON OF THE FRONTIER
IN AUSTRALIA AND THE UNITED STATES

H. C. ALLEN

Commonwealth Fund Professor of American History
in the University of London

ANGUS & ROBERTSON
Sydney · London · Wellington · Melbourne

MICHIGAN STATE UNIVERSITY PRESS

1959

To Mary

PREFACE

MY OBJECT in writing this essay—it is no more than that—was to look a little at the way in which Frederick Jackson Turner's frontier thesis might be broadly applied to another continent and society than the North American. It draws no grandiose conclusions and, indeed, pretends to do nothing except to stimulate thought, and perhaps suggest one or two lines of approach to a subject which has already received some attention, as, of late years, it has come to be seen increasingly as an international and not merely an American phenomenon.

I should like to tender my warm thanks to the many friends who have given me the benefit of their advice, and, in particular, to Dr. R. M. Hartwell, Mr. L. H. Fitzhardinge, Professor O. H. K. Spate, and Dr. J. R. Pole. I should like to thank Dr. Russel Ward for the stimulus of his ideas about Australian folk ballads, and for permission to quote from his work on the subject. I should like, finally, to express my appreciation to Sir Keith Hancock for reading through a draft of the manuscript, and for giving me his comments and support. The responsibility for the many shortcomings of the book is entirely mine.

It was really made possible by a nine-month visit to the Australian National University in Canberra as a Senior Research Fellow in 1953-54. I wish to acknowledge with gratitude my debt to the University, its officials and members, for this opportunity, not merely to make this little study, but also for the vivid experience of getting to know something of their great land— *Terra Australis,* to me hitherto veritably *Incognita*.

H. C. ALLEN

CHESHAM BOIS,
  BUCKS.
February, 1959

CONTENTS

CONTENTS

INTRODUCTION

THREE MOTIVES have gone to the making of this subject. First is a conviction that comparative historical studies have been unwarrantably neglected by academic historians. History is the record of past events which are unique, and we historians cannot repeat its great experiments as in a laboratory. But this does not mean that we cannot look at history in the same way that certain scientists, geologists for instance, look at nature; and in such cases history and science have this in common, that they can in reality only proceed by testing their hypotheses against sets of facts which are given and, in so far as they are correct, unalterable. Thus it may well be that comparative studies of similar historical phenomena may lead to valid and valuable conclusions about the nature of the historical process.[1]

It is not to be expected that we shall by this method arrive at any "laws of nature" as sweeping and yet as exact as those of the physical sciences, but we should not forget that the general laws of some of the biological sciences are less precise; and when we turn to psychology—if science it be—there seems little theoretical reason why its probabilities should be much more predictable than those of history. A comparison of only two frontier areas is not a full test of the method, for conclusions must be few and limited; but we may derive something from it which we could not obtain from two unitary studies.[2]

The second motive which lies behind this choice of subject is my inclination to believe that in a pioneer environment we can most easily study the fundamental springs of human action. Even though we must beware of dangerously oversimplified and overgeneralized conceptions of both Man and Nature, we can perhaps still claim that when we are observing man on the frontier we are seeing him with all that is inessential shorn away, seeing him, so to speak, stripped for battle with elemental forces. To enable him to grapple with the wilderness, he has perforce to reduce his needs, and so his problems, to their rudiments, though because he is civilized man and not primitive, he regards this as a temporary phase; he is not there to come to terms with the outback, as his native predecessors tended to do, but to conquer it in the name of civilization. This sustained effort to subjugate nature, which is the essence of the frontier, is a dramatic and absorbing saga for the historian, under whose full scrutiny —in the case of some of the more recent peoples—the whole process may fall. Thus, a comparative frontier study offers one of our best hopes of illuminating that relationship of man to his environment, which is a central problem for geographers and historians, but which cannot be profitably considered by either without the aid of the other.

My third motive for choosing this subject is an interest in testing the validity of the frontier hypothesis itself. While reflecting upon the controversy which has been waged over the Turner thesis, as any historian of America must, it occurred to me, as it has to others,[3] that light might be thrown on the matter by a comparative study. If similar conditions elsewhere produced, or failed to produce, similar results to those claimed by historians of Turner's school, their conclusions might be correspondingly strengthened or weakened. The country or area which should be chosen ought, it seemed to me, to be as similar as possible to America in its natural and its human circumstances, but at the same time ought not to be too subject to the influence of the United States, for this would constitute a major complicating factor. Plainly, if we are interested in seeing whether, in similar circumstances, a similar environment produces similar reactions in its inhabitants, we must as far as possible avoid cases of direct imitation, whether conscious or unconscious.[4] For this reason, Canada, otherwise an obvious choice, had to be ruled out.

Australia, on the other hand, has sufficient in common with the United States, geographically and historically, to make comparison possible, but has not been anything like so greatly influenced by her as Canada. Of course, there has been considerable American influence, as there has on most countries of the world in the twentieth century, and it is markedly on the increase. There were persistent, and at first very important, trans-Pacific contacts from the earliest times,[5] and in the days of the Australian gold rushes, which followed hard on the heels of those in California, there was a considerable migration of miners. With the coming of Australian democratic self-government, there was a distinct tendency to look to the example set by the great American continental democracy. The federal system of the Australian Commonwealth, which came into effect in 1901, owed more to the Constitution of the United States than to any other; and some Australians even looked forward for a while to the advent of the "United States of Australia."[6] In manifold other things, often small in themselves, Australia owed much to America; thus the universal ax in use in Australia—symbol almost of the bushman, as it is of the frontiersman—is the American ax,[7] which seems to have been brought first to the gold fields in the fifties, and which is different from the old English ax.[8] Yet it should be possible to distinguish the principal American importations and imitations from the native developments of the Australian frontier, since there are, for all their similarities, many striking differences between the histories of the American and Australian peoples and of the characteristics and institutions which they have developed.

Other historians, of course, have given thought to this question. One Australian has directly considered the application of the American theme to his country's history;[9] another has brilliantly applied it to certain aspects of the development of the British Commonwealth as a whole;[10] two Canadians have used it with great skill, one in the course of a very successful specimen of the comparative study, and the other in an essay in a most interesting volume by a number of historians on the frontiers in many lands and ages;[11] yet others have contributed to it.[12] But, to the best of my knowledge, no historian[13] primarily interested in America has made a deliberate, and at least semisystematic, attempt to compare the frontier thesis in its application to Australia and the United States. Possibly this is because of the continental isolation of so much American history, the sense of which is peculiarly strong in historians of the American frontier; Turner, after all, was in reaction from an excessive concentration among the American historians of his day upon the Germanic origins of American institutions.[14]

In essence, then, we are to study the history of man in the environment of two untamed lands of continental extent. I propose first, therefore, to consider for a brief moment the relationship of the two histories in time; next, to compare the environments and the peoples environed; then to contrast the way those peoples made their living; and after that to attempt a comparison of the effects of their frontier environment upon them. In the end, it may be possible to cast a gleam of light upon the validity of the frontier thesis, and even finally to hazard an observation or two upon the nature of man's relationship to his environment.

Toynbee maintains that, for purposes of comparison, civilizations may be regarded as "philosophically contemporaneous,"[15] and even in the actual historical time-scale of civilizations the American and Australian frontiers are approximately contemporary: for a substantial period they were precisely concurrent. The first American colony was founded in 1607; Australia, in 1788; the American frontier is generally reckoned to have been open until 1890, and the Australian frontier at least as long, so that the two have a whole century of history in common. But it was America's third century and Australia's first, which makes a distinct difference. In any earlier age the difference might not have been very important, but Australia was born at the opening of that phenomenal development of man's technological control over nature which we inadequately describe as the Industrial Revolution. Its "stupendous energies"[16] make comparisons between her first century and that of America unjust, without rendering comparisons between them from 1788 onward any fairer. It was the Industrial Revolution which enabled Australia, despite natural disadvantages *vis-à-vis* America, to grow to a population of eight million after one hundred and sixty years, whereas the United States had not reached four million after one hundred and eighty years. That Australian eight million in 1950, however, was overshadowed altogether by America's one hundred and fifty million.

If, however, we make the necessary allowances for this fact, the two frontiers can be regarded as not incomparable in time.

BUSH AND BACKWOODS

1: *Geography*

THE TWO CONTINENTAL domains of Australia and the United States are equal in extent, being almost exactly three million square miles in area. Nor are they altogether dissimilar in shape, the main difference being that the St. Lawrence-Great Lakes system and the Gulf of Mexico have had the effect, given the main direction of American settlement, of compressing United States energies into the Westward Movement. This movement of peoples has been of peculiar importance in American growth.

Being in the northern hemisphere, the United States lies opposite the European land mass, the peoples of whose western seaboard led the way both in overseas migration and in the great technological advances which have been the peculiar contribution of the West to man's development. Australia, on the other hand, amid her wastes of southern waters, has been quite eccentric to the expansion of the European peoples, whose technical supremacy alone has rendered it possible for them to occupy this distant land, lying as it does on the southern threshold of that part of Asia which has long contained so high a proportion of the world's population.

The more central position of the United States in the world, as compared with that of Australia, is indicated by the fact that it is 3,000 nautical miles from New York to Liverpool, and 4,500 from San Francisco to Yokohama, whereas, though it is not far from Darwin to Indonesia, it is by sea 4,700 miles from Perth to Capetown, 9,550 miles from Perth to London through Suez, and 6,550 miles from Sydney to San Francisco via Suva and Honolulu. What is more, compared with Australia, the United States is, as it were, on the way to many places (as phenomena so seemingly disparate as Columbus' voyages and modern air routes illustrate). This Australia is not. The north Atlantic is

3

the main sea highway of the world, and, even in the northern Pacific, Americans participated in a flourishing Oriental trade before the continental United States came into political existence.[1]

The American frontier, indeed, has enjoyed in its history the best of two worlds. Central enough to be directly in the path of European overseas expansion, it has been sufficiently isolated[2] to afford it very considerable protection, while not, as in the case of Australia, being so cut off as to constitute a serious hindrance to development. The challenge of France and Spain was a stimulus, and probably a beneficial one, in early years; but they ceased to be a serious threat by the date of the separation from Britain, and she herself ceased to be a menace after 1814, by which time the United States was unrivaled in the Western Hemisphere. Neither Australia nor the United States has been seriously threatened by foreign powers until the twentieth century, largely because of the existence of the *Pax Britannica* in the nineteenth. They have equally, though Australia more overtly, been beneficiaries, not only of their geographical insularity, but of the power and benevolence of the Royal Navy.

This underlines the importance of the sea in the development of the two countries. In view of the significance of the coastal trade to the United States before the middle of the nineteenth century, Australia might seem to have enjoyed a considerable natural advantage in her island position. Yet America has a great maritime tradition, which Australia, having been perhaps too long reliant on that of the mother country, really has not.[3] For the United States, the very barrier of Panama acted as a powerful incentive to open up land routes across the Great Plains and the mountains to the Pacific coast, and eventually, of course, to build the canal itself. No comparable spur to the opening of the difficult interior of Australia existed, so that ease of coastal transportation may have been a disadvantage in disguise.[4]

The actual manner of settlement in the two lands greatly

emphasized this difference. The United States, broadly speaking, was settled from that of her coasts which lies nearest to Europe on direct ocean routes; her frontier moved forward from the three main centers of Virginia, New England, and the Middle Colonies, incorporating or elbowing aside the alien settlements edging up from the Gulf of Mexico and down from Canada. The Americans, after building up their combined strength behind the protective barrier of the Appalachians,[5] surged inexorably westward, overleaping the physical barriers of the Southwest and seizing the fertile and attractive lands bordering the Pacific. Only in its final stages, consequent upon the series of precious metal discoveries in the Far West which began in California in 1848, was this westward flood met by any substantial movement eastward from the Pacific coast, on the part of settlers who had gone there around the Horn or across Central America.[6]

Australia, on the other hand, was settled from east, south, west, and even north. The first settlement at Port Jackson (Sydney) in 1788 was on the southeastern coast, the most distant one from Britain. The next settlement, which was made from this mother colony of New South Wales in 1803, was also in the southeast, in Tasmania. The third, at Moreton Bay (or what was later to be Brisbane in Queensland), was also a military convict settlement made by sea from Sydney in 1824, as was the abortive foundation at Melville Island in the extreme north, near the present-day Darwin, in the same year. The next, on the Swan River in Western Australia where Perth now stands, was made from the United Kingdom and was more logically sited geographically, but it was ill-conceived in other ways and made extremely slow progress for half a century. That in Victoria in 1834, though it became a natural and swiftly growing offspring of New South Wales, was made initially by sea (from Tasmania), as was the colony at Adelaide in South Australia, which was founded from the mother country in 1836 and which alone of the first foundations never had convict labor. Not until 1864 was a permanent, though long precarious,

5

settlement made at Darwin, one of the points in Australia nearest to the rest of mankind; and even then it was actually made,
anomalous as it may seem, from Adelaide and by sea.

Thus, Australia was settled from a number of widely sep-
arated centers, whence men radiated out into the heart of the
continent, and these centers themselves were not, before 1901,
effectively bound together politically at any lesser level then remote London.[7] Australia never had a frontier; the most that can
be said is that she had a number of them, and even this is often
denied.[8] As Miles Franklin put it, "Australia never had a frontier. She had an outback . . ."[9] Outback! the very word has a
ring of dispersed remoteness from the centers of civilization; it
is the "scarce-explored Outside Country—Death-o'-Day, Back-
o'-Beyond—all the lone Never Never . . . ,"[10] and those who
call it so are conscious that beyond it there lies the so-called
"dead heart" of Australia. This is a very different thing from
the phrase "back country," which has been its nearest equivalent in American history. This is of the greatest interest, for it
expresses the sense of remorseless movement which underlies
the concept of the American frontier; it is not only a single,
predominant frontier but also a moving one. Australia has not
only had a number of frontiers, but none, save for a period the
pastoral frontier of New South Wales, has had anything except
a remote affinity with the perennial drive of the American
people to the West, which swept Britain, France, Spain, Russia,
and Mexico out of their path to its Pacific seaboard.

Australia has been less well endowed by nature than
America, which is indeed of all nations probably the richest in
natural resources, whereas Australia has justly been called "the
last-found and least-favoured of continents."[11] One reason for
this is that Australia, on the whole, is more homogeneous in
climate and terrain than the United States. But the principal
reason is that it is a dry continent; aridity is the transcendent
difficulty of Australia, and almost all her ills are connected with
and subsidiary to it. No less than eighty-seven percent of the

continent has an average annual rainfall of less than 30 inches,[12] much of it very unreliable.[13] More than a half of the United States, but only about a third of Australia, has a better rainfall than 20 inches a year, whereas something of the order of a third of America has more than 40 inches compared with only one tenth approximately of Australia. The contrast is neatly exemplified in the fact that the United States has about five times as much temperate land with a rainfall of over 20 inches as Australia, and Australia about five times as much arid country with a rainfall of less than 10 inches as America.

This aridity is aggravated by temperature control, for Australia is also warm, falling as it does, with the exception of Tasmania, entirely between the 10th and 40th parallels, compared with the 20th and 50th parallels in the case of the United States. Evaporation rates are therefore high throughout Australia, and not much even of its tropical area is wet. None of the United States is actually in the Tropics, and very high evaporation coincides with low precipitation in only one area, the Southwest. On the other hand, Australia is very free from frost and snow, though this is not a sufficient compensation for inadequate water.

The situation is further aggravated by Australia's lack of mountains. Only about one fourteenth of Australia, compared with about one third of the United States, is higher than 2,000 feet. The eastern coastal range of Australia is comparable in position and size with the Appalachians, the highest peaks reaching 6,000 and 7,000 feet respectively. But whereas these are the highest mountains in Australia, in the West of the United States there looms the majestic Cordillera system, attaining in places a height of 14,000 feet. Australia's only other two little mountain groups, in central and western Australia, are hardly worthy of the name. This not only means more evaporation and less snow, but also little precipitation of rain.

The only source of water, therefore, in which Australia is rich is underground, for she has the largest artesian basin in the world. This has proved of the greatest value to the pastoral industry, but it has not realized all that was once hoped of it, which is also true of the artesian waters of the American Southwest, which have been an equal disappointment. The exact quantity of Australia's underground reserves is still uncertain, and only about one fourth of her arid region can be ameliorated by artesian water, much of which is, in any case, saline.

The crux of Australia's aridity problem is its lack of first-rate river systems. Splendid rivers run down to the sea from the eastern coastal range, but they are very much shorter than their counterparts on the eastern coastal plain of the United States, which is more extensive than its Australian counterpart. There are some good coastal rivers in the north, but the only continental system is that of the Murray, which has a drainage area of about half a million square miles, as compared with the Mississippi Basin of approximately one and a quarter million square miles.[14] One of the Murray's chief tributaries, the Murrumbidgee, occasionally fails to reach it, and it has itself ceased to flow in three separate years of drought. The comparison with the great American rivers was aptly expressed by Henry Lawson in a story of a "Yankee who was invited up to Bourke to report on a proposed scheme for locking the river . . . They led him to the Darling [main tributary of the Murray], and he had a look at it . . . 'Look here, fellows,' he drawled, . . . 'I'll tell you what I'll dew. I'll bottle that damned river of yourn in twenty-four hours!' "[15] This grievous lack of rivers in the heart of the continent is perhaps Australia's greatest single handicap. Even the rivers of the American Southwest, such as the Colorado, which the Murray most resembles, are much superior to it because they spring from great mountains. The handicap to irrigation is shown by the fact that the Missouri and Columbia basins in 1937 irrigated approximately four million acres each, the Colorado Basin two and a half million acres, and even the Rio Grande Basin one and a half million, whereas the quota of the Murray was about five hundred thousand acres.[16] But beyond this, in the history of the Australian frontier compared with that of the United States, the lack of large-scale, navigable inland waterways has been a decisive deterrent to development. Old Man River is not a conceivable figure in Australian folklore.

Australia's soils, too, are on the whole poor, and more than half of its total area "contains scarcely any land fit for agriculture and very little fit for pastoralism of any degree of intensity."[17] There is really nothing at all comparable to the wonderful lands of the great Mississippi Valley, but once again it is Australia's misfortune that the area of chief soil deposition, from the Gulf of Carpentaria to the Murray mouth, is too dry for dense agricultural settlement; as Griffith Taylor puts it, "if the desert of central Australia could be replaced by" a "warm sea, like the Gulf of Mexico, just to the south,"[18] the history of Australia would be markedly different.

Fauna and flora are similarly affected by the aridity and the conditions which produce it. The richness and multiformity of American animal life are quite unmatched in Australia. The predominant marsupials, particularly the kangaroo, are of far less value than, for instance, were the buffaloes of the Great Plains, though it seems that this poverty of fauna is due to the natural history rather than the geological nature of Australia, for a number of imported species have flourished. The Indian buffalo, not to be confused with the American bison, has formed great herds in the Northern Territory, and the rabbit rapidly became—until the advent of myxomatosis—Australia's primary pest. But nonetheless, in the Winter Range area of the United States it takes 75 acres to pasture one steer; in the Sparselands of the Northern Territory, 640 acres. Forests in Australia are scanty compared with the vast, heavily timbered areas of the United States in its natural state; in a great coastal belt, nearly all round the continent, eucalypts are predominant but seldom heavily concentrated, and within that belt at the core of the land is a large tract where the scattered acacia prevails. There is nothing to approach the great American variety of natural vegetation.

In the heart of Australia is the dead land of fixed dunes, and Australia has about a million square miles of desert and semi-desert to America's 200,000. Griffith Taylor divides Australia into two unequal parts; the smaller, which he calls *Economic Australia,* consists of the area contained by a crude arc drawn at a radius of some five hundred miles round Perth, along with a belt which includes a small southeastern corner of South Australia, Victoria, nearly all of New South Wales, and a corresponding strip of eastern Queensland as far north as Cooktown; the remainder of the continent he calls *Empty Australia.* It is as if all the land between the Appalachians and the 100th meridian had been left out of the United States; for it is only 450 miles from Sydney west to the beginning of the arid zone.[19] The northwestern half of the whole Australian continent contains less than one half of one percent of the population of the country.

Mineral resources alone are unaffected by climate, but Australia has hitherto been found greatly wanting in oil, while its coal and base-metal deposits are not among the world's largest. But in those commodities which are the staples of the miner's frontier, she is rich; her silver, and above all her gold deposits have been large and have been most influential in the country's development. Its uranium resources are proving important, and the Rum Jungle mine may yet begin a new era which will at long last decisively advance Australia's final and obdurate frontier in the Northern Territory.

Even those intrepid leaders of the frontier, the explorers, who much resemble one another in the two lands,[20] had on the whole a far harder time of it in Australia. The Americans had more obvious hazards, Indians, great rivers, huge mountain ranges, winter blizzards, but the Australians had no water; again and again, struggling against what A. G. L. Shaw calls Australia's two great enemies, "too little water and too much distance,"[21] they met disaster. Only the Spaniards in the Southwest and later pioneers in the same area underwent the same hardships and ran the same risks, and in a sense they had more to gain, for the irony of Australian exploration, and indeed of the Australian frontier, has been that the lands which were opened up with such prodigious effort proved largely sterile. Australia is essentially still a land peopled upon the perimeter and empty within, and as a result almost every center of importance can to this day be reached by sea. The lot of America's explorers was not disillusion like that of Australia's, for they had a more certain objective: their Promised Land on the Pacific coast was a reality. They long believed that their path was blocked by an obstacle as formidable as the dead heart of Australia, the Great American Desert (as the Great Plains were called in the first half of the nineteenth century), but, though it contained a certain element of truth, that belief was to a considerable degree an illusion; the Great Australian Desert was not. And in any case, the lush territory of Oregon, the fertile valleys of California, and the rich metal resources of the Cordillera region made America's arid lands well worth crossing. Perth or Darwin could readily be visited by swift ship, and the only transcontinental railway, from Adelaide to Perth, crosses the Nullarbor Plain within much less than one hundred miles of the Great Australian Bight, while the toil, tears, and sweat—and money—that have gone to the linking of Adelaide with far-off, tiny Darwin has produced no through means of communication overland except a telegraph line; for the rest, a twice-a-week railway runs north as far as Alice Springs, after which a strategic road takes on the very limited traffic that there is.

Verily has Australia been called the Cinderella of the continents. Although they do not represent his final and considered judgment, the words of an Australian character of Henry Lawson's have a certain air of verisimilitude about them:

The worst and hardest years of my life were spent in Australia . . . I worked harder and got less in my own country in five

years than I ever did in any other in fifteen . . . No, Australia is
the worst country that ever the Lord had the sense to forget. I
mean to stick to the country that stuck to me, when I was
starved out of my own dear native land—and that country is
the United States of America. What's Australia? A big, thirsty,
hungry wilderness, with one or two cities for the convenience of
foreign speculators . . . Why, the Australians haven't even got
the grit to claim enough of their own money to throw a few
dams across their watercourses, and so make some of the interior
fit to live in. America's bad enough, but it was never so small
as that . . .[22]

This judgment is not only unjust to Australia, but even a little
unfair to the United States. America has been singularly blessed
by nature, though her critics, and even her friends, have often
laid too much emphasis on her resources and too little on the
genius her people have displayed in exploiting them. The American frontier was not a soulless phenomenon impelled by the
vast forces of history: it was peopled and kept moving by men
and women of flesh and blood and good sense and manifold
skills and superabundant energy.

But it is nonetheless true that the Americans' struggle with
nature was, for the most part, far more rewarding than that of
the Australians. America's good fortune extended, indeed, beyond the richness of her material means in a way not often remarked, for she was uniquely lucky in the timing and placing
of her development. Observe this element of happy chance in
the dynamic advance of her frontier. Observe how the British
entered this continent of ultimately fabulous riches at what ap-
peared too late an hour for the treasure troves, and how their
advance was apparently frustrated, but in the long run facil-
itated, by the coastal mountains, while the French and the
Spaniards over-extended themselves westward to their ultimate
cost. See how the great river system of the Mississippi aided
their swift rush down the western slopes of the mountains to
the river itself, and then see, at the moment when oar and
paddle and sail and current were becoming inadequate, how

the steam engine, invented in distant England, and applied in Europe and America to ship propulsion, not only revolutionized the bulk and speed of river traffic, but made upstream movement easy, thus opening up the long Missouri and the other limited stretches of navigable river to the west of the Mississippi. See again, at this critical moment, when the waves of Westward Movement were breaking on the shores of the Great American Desert and when many of the ablest Americans—the so-called limitationists—believed that the United States had reached its natural boundaries, how the discovery of gold provided a supreme incentive (in addition to attractive lands) for leaping across or around the desert wastes, which then began to turn out not to be so barren after all. Mark, above all, how at this juncture other inventions, originated and also developed in Europe—such as the steam engine, the locomotive, and the railway—were ready for Americans, so that they were able to subdue their last frontier and build their continental empire. Other nations, such as Britain, have had good fortune in their history, but none perhaps such good fortune as this; small wonder that the Westward Movement of the American frontier has had many of the unique qualities that it has.

The diversity of American resources and of American frontier experience meant that the frontier left a heritage behind it as it moved on, the geographical sections: "As the successive Wests became Easts a mosaic of sections was left behind, each bent on shaping national legislation to its own ends."[23] Because of the relative homogeneity of the Australian environment and population, its national divisions, despite its long history of colonial separation, are but a pale image of the American; they do, however, exist. Before federation in 1901 there was a powerful secessionist movement in Northern Queensland; after it, Western Australia, which can be regarded as a surviving frontier-state, has shown distinct, if sporadic signs of discontent; and there is at the present time a strong movement for the creation of a new state in the New England of

Australia (that is, the northern section of New South Wales). But certainly Australian sectionalism has not led, and is most unlikely to lead, to such agonizing tension as that which resulted in the American Civil War.

But a consideration of American sectionalism does suggest that there is one American geographical region which is extraordinarily similar to the whole of Australia, and that is the West, particularly the Great Plains and the Southwest. Despite obvious differences of size, elevation, and latitude, the area of the Dakotas, Nebraska, Kansas, Oklahoma, Texas, Montana, Wyoming, Colorado, New Mexico, Utah, Arizona, Nevada, and California is very like Australia in structure and climate.[24] A glance, for instance, at a map of the mean annual temperature of the world shows that the 70° F. isotherm, which, in the Southern Hemisphere, runs pretty much east to west through the heart of Australia, in the Northern Hemisphere runs through Florida at about Daytona Beach and across the northern waters of the Gulf south of Louisiana approximately to Galveston, at which point it turns dramatically northwest in a great loop the top of which curves around the Great Salt Lake, and thus descends to the mouth of the California River, and thence to a point a little west of the southern tip of Lower California, whereupon it resumes its western tenor. The soil of this great area is akin to, and even the vegetation is not wildly dissimilar from, that of Australia.

The parallels between the areas are manifold. On the vital water question, for instance,[25] the Australian saying that the "Government is not leasing land but *rainfall* to the settlers"[26] may be compared with the words of J. W. Powell's famous report on the *Lands of the Arid Region,* "Monopoly of land need not be feared. The question for legislators to solve is to devise some practicable means by which water rights may be distributed among individual farmers . . ."[27] The advances and retreats of settlers in Kansas over the 96th or 98th meridians in the second half of the nineteenth century were extraordinarily

14

like those of South Australians over Surveyor Goyder's Line of safe settlement in the same period. Other natural hazards are remarkably similar too; scorching winds and soil erosion, droughts and floods, bush and forest fires, even plagues of grasshoppers (to say nothing of the ubiquitous fly) were present in both lands to daunt the settler.[28] The staple diet of the cowboy on the trail—steer beef or bacon, campfire biscuits and black coffee—is the counterpart of that of the Australian bushman—mutton or salt beef, campfire damper, and milkless tea. The sod house of the Great Plains, too, was matched by the primitive home-station of bark or sods, which was sometimes the first residence of the Australian squatter. There is even a likeness between the attitude of Australians to the continent in which they live, their emphasis on its impersonal antiquity—it has been called the Timeless Land—and the changed attitude of the Americans to their habitat when they reached the West, and there acquired a stronger feeling for their own newness and for the immemorial age of the plains and mountains. Over and over again we shall see this likeness between Australia and the West, and between the effect that both produced upon their first inhabitants of European origin. The famous injunction, for instance, to the farmers of Kansas to raise less corn and more hell has a very Australian ring about it.

But this particular likeness between Australia and the West, and the many differences between the United States and Australia as a whole, must not cause us to forget the broad similarities between these two great, and by European standards, unsettled, lands of approximately equal extent, containing areas of great fertility but many natural hazards, and long protected from the shocks of international affairs by Britain's navy and their own insularity.

2: *Peoples*

THE INHABITANTS of the two countries, likewise, have some dissimilarities but many likenesses, and this is particularly true of the white settlers.

The Australian people, like their geographical surroundings, are far more homogeneous, in racial and national origin, than the American. Thus, in 1947—there was a marked difference in policy in the postwar decade—of all Australians, excepting 47,000 full blood aborigines, 99.3 percent were of unmixed European stock, whereas in 1940 only 89.4 percent of Americans were white. Of the few nonwhite Australians, the principal groups were about 9,000 Chinese and 5,000 Polynesians; of the non-European Americans approximately 13 million were Negro, 334,000 American Indian, 127,000 Japanese, and 78,-000 Chinese.[1]

Similarly, of the persons resident in Australia in 1947, 99.5 percent were British, about 99 percent of them born in the British Commonwealth. This does not mean that the long-standing Australian boast of being "98 percent British" was true in the sense of their being of British stock; such estimates are necessarily crude, but it is likely that at that time some 90 percent of them were of British origin. This, it may be noted, is a proportion very similar to that of the American people who were of British origin at the end of the colonial period. Nor should it be forgotten that the immigration quota system introduced after World War I in the United States, and still in operation, was deliberately devised to maintain the predominance of northern European stocks in the American population. When, however, we compare the numbers of foreign-born in the two countries, as for instance in 1933 in Australia and 1930 in the United States, when the figure for both was some-

16

what over 10 percent, we must not lose sight of the fact that a
high proportion of the Australians in question were British-
born.

There is no denying the importance of this fact. Australians,
as a whole, are, and for the most part always have been, belligerently proud of their British ancestry and of their connection
with the British Commonwealth, though this does not for a
moment mean that they are, or wish to be, like the inhabitants
of the United Kingdom. True, there was a potent republican
and nationalist movement in Australia in the last years of the
nineteenth century—there was after all audible republicanism
in England in its middle years—but the federation effectively
put an end to it; it was indeed hard for British colonies to break
violently away from the mother country once she became determined to let them depart in peace. The contrast with the
American experience is plain; it was indeed one of the principal
reasons for the British change of heart toward her colonial
dependencies. But it certainly remains true, in the words of
Hancock, that "if such a creature as the average Briton exists
anywhere upon this earth, he will be found in Australia."[2]

The largest nonwhite group in the United States, the Negroes,
can hardly, in view of their origin in the slave trade, simply be
called settlers, and they do furnish the most startling contrast
with the composition of the Australian population; in fact, they
were one of the chief reasons for the determined Australian re-
jection of nonwhite immigration. Numbering three quarters of
a million in 1790, they increased to nearly thirteen million by
1940. They have had, of course, and are still having, a profound effect upon the United States as a whole, but particularly
upon the South where they are mostly concentrated even yet,
for it was in part their existence that made of the Southern
frontier the peculiar phenomenon it was.

On the other hand, Oriental settlement provides striking
parallels between the two countries: Chinese have been present

in considerable numbers in both, Japanese in substantial numbers in America, and Indians in some numbers in Australia. Each country, too, has had a special immigration problem, Kanakas in Australia, Mexicans in the United States. The numbers in all these groups proportionate to the total populations are not widely different. That this is so is partly due to the similar circumstances of their arrival; both countries began to receive Orientals on a large scale first in the gold fields; in both there was, in due course, a strong reaction; and in both exclusion by one means or another was eventually enforced. The problems have remained manageable in both because of the exclusion policy.

But the contrast provided by the Negro problem remains. Australia is firmly committed to the White Australia policy, America to at least a biracial democracy. The South, of course, swiftly as it has moved in the last decade, remains a question mark; it, after all, largely invented the literacy tests and poll taxes by which nonwhites have been excluded from Australia. In the history of the Australian frontier there is no such cleavage as existed between the slave and free frontiers of the United States before 1860.

This does not mean that there was no source of servile labor in Australia, even if there were no slaves as such, for this was precisely the function performed by the convicts who constituted in the early years so important and large a part of Australian settlement. It was the loss of the American colonies which prompted the foundation of a penal colony at Botany Bay, but transported felons had formed a very insignificant element in the population of what was to be the United States, numbering perhaps somewhere between twenty-five and fifty thousand in all in a population of four million at the end of the colonial period.[3] Very different was the proportion of convicts to free men in Australia, where approximately 160,000 arrived before the abolition of "transportation" in the middle years of the nineteenth century; of these about 150,000 were absorbed into the eastern states, whose population hardly exceeded 400,000 at the close of the epoch. Emancipated convicts formed a sizeable portion of the original Australian stock.

From the point of view of the frontier, they were important as a fund of cheap labor, far more so than the indentured servants of the American colonies, whom they also resembled in some respects. But they were, in reality, much more like the slaves; they had not the latter's ineradicable badge of color, but they bore in practice a moral stigma which the slave did not. That their children were born free was the saving grace of Australia and the opportunity for one of her most remarkable achievements: "They sent us the sweepings of England, and the sun and the earth made men of them in half a century. Out of despair and brutality we built the beginnings of democracy . . ."[4]

The penal origins of Australia were indeed so gloomy that contemporaries were fully aware of the analogy with the slave system.[5] The likeness between conditions on convict transports and on slave ships was the subject of remark, and mortality rates were often comparable; the feasibility of the segregation of the sexes on convict vessels was actually defended on the ground that it was the practice on slavers. Nor did the resemblance cease at dock side: bad conditions, gang labor, the use of chains—symbol almost of slavery—were common to the two. Above all, the savagery of discipline, the brutalizing effect of the frequent use of the lash on both giver and receiver, was a bond the systems shared. The blood drawn by the lash in Australia was not to be paid for by more blood drawn with the sword, but who can count the cost of such a system and its degrading effect upon the nation which received these outcasts? It is hard to believe that these scenes over which we still prefer to draw a veil—"the blood of the victims bespattering the surroundings", the "swollen, gangrened, fly-blown backs stuck to their shirts"[6]—can have been without their effect.

19

In some respects the slave and convict frontiers, both of which, be it remembered, owed their first beginnings to Great Britain, have left their mark to this day. The problem of the Negro and the South is plain for all to see, but there has been much dispute in Australia about the degree of convict influence in Australian history. The issue was a live one in politics for the first half century of her existence in the form of a struggle between the "exclusives" and the "emancipists," the always free against the one-time bond. After that it tended for many years to be a genealogical, before it became an historical, question, with much ink, naturally enough, spent in an effort to demonstrate how small a percentage of Australians had any convict blood in their veins,[7] an effort which was successful, for there is little doubt that the number is not so very large. But in a sense this dispute really misses the point, for in these conditions heredity may count for little and environment for much. What men are is often less important than what they think they are or ought to be, and what they think they are is to a large degree determined by the circumstances and prevailing ideas amidst which they are reared and live. Russel Ward has recently shown the importance of convict influence in *The Australian Legend,* and it is now possible to go somewhat further than Hancock was prepared to do twenty-five years ago: "Yet we may suspect that there has come down to us, by subtle hidden channels, a vague unmeasured inheritance from those early days."[8]

The link between immigration and the frontier is not always direct. From the middle of the nineteenth century onward in the United States, and even earlier in Australia, there was a marked tendency for immigrants to go to the great cities. This development accompanied increased urbanization, and Australia has always been more highly urbanized than the United States. Even though the bases on which the figures are calculated may not be precisely the same, they are illuminating. In 1850 over 20 percent of the Australians lived in towns, as compared with 15 percent of the Americans; in 1947 and 1950 the figures were 69 percent and 59 percent, respectively. Here plainly is a contrast of great importance in the history of the frontiers, and it is made even more significant by the extraordinarily high proportion of Australians who live in the great metropolises, for as early as 1835 over a quarter of the population of New South Wales lived in Sydney, while in 1947 over a half of all Australians lived in the six capital cities. This we shall see to be of the utmost consequence—to take one instance—in the fact that Australian radicalism has had, not so much rural, as urban roots. But even where immigrants did not go direct to the frontiers, the pressure of immigration in both countries has been of notable significance in providing a labor pool and an expanding population which pushed the limits of settlement onward.

Moreover, the flow of immigration to the two lands has remarkable similarities. In the United States in the years before World War I, when it was greatest, it was effected without direct state aid. In Australia, because costs were so much higher owing to the distances involved, such aid has nearly always been necessary to promote large-scale movement; and since 1945 the Australian government has supported immigration on a quite unprecedented scale, with the surprising result that Australia in the ten years following World War II absorbed immigrants at a greater rate proportionate to its total population than the United States has ever done.[9] Between 1945 and 1955 she accepted more than one million immigrants,[10] or an average of a hundred thousand a year. It should be noted, too, that the character of this immigration has changed, for only just under half have been British in origin. Thus the proportion of the persons resident in Australia who are British subjects has sunk from 99.5 percent in 1947 to 95.5 percent in 1954. This has not been without effects similar to those displayed in nineteenth century American Nativism, though in a milder form, for there is some measure of feeling against the so-called

"New Australians." However, despite the rate of Australian immigration, the salient fact remains that the prodigious flood of American immigration up to World War I directly and indirectly gave to the Westward Movement much of its peculiar impetus.

Once again one must not lose sight of basic similarities. The populations were largely European in origin, with the important exception of the Negroes, for other alien races were, in one way or another, prevented from entering in large numbers. What is more, they were predominantly of northern European stock, and in both cases the largest single immigrant group was the English-speaking.[11] This group, in each case, brought with it much in the way of political and social tradition besides the language that is common to both Australia and the United States.

So much for the settlers, but what of the indigenous inhabitants? They were on the wrong side of the frontier, part, as it seemed to the frontiersmen, of the wilderness which they were striving to subdue, and were treated accordingly. Looking back, we can see that they were the tragic victims of the remorseless processes of history. Their defeat was certain: the question is whether it might not have been less ruthless. In this respect it is hard to choose between the Australian and American frontiers, even though the Australian blackfellow was very different from the American redskin. The former had developed a system, specialized and in some ways complex, which enabled him to live in the difficult conditions of the Australian Bush; but by European standards it was exceedingly primitive from both the economic and military standpoints. This meant that they were capable of sporadic violence but not of tribal war as America understood it, which put the approximately 300,000 aborigines peculiarly at the mercy of the white man, and in the case of the perhaps 2,500 native Tasmanians the brutal result was absolute extinction within seventy-five years of the first settlement on the island.

The American Indian, too, superior though he was in war to the aborigine, was at a great technical disadvantage against the forces of Europe, but among the 850,000 who are estimated to have inhabited the present territory of the United States in the seventeenth century, there were more, and more variegated, ways of life than existed among the aborigines in their relatively homogeneous environment. The "timber" Indians of the East, the Indians of the Great Plains, and the Pueblo Indians of the Southwest, to name but three groups, differed greatly in their modes of existence, but all were better fitted for their ordeal by civilization than the original inhabitants of Australia; only perhaps in the Digger Indians of California, living, like the aborigines, upon the roots, grubs, and other scanty natural products of their arid habitat, and like them in little more than family units, is there anything approaching a parallel with Australia. The great majority had an effective tribal organization, and reveled in the pursuit of war; in this they much more closely resembled the Bantu of South Africa or, above all, the Maori of New Zealand than the Australian aborigine.

Yet the Indians were increasingly unable to withstand the onrush of the frontier. At first they were a grave threat to the settlers, because they outnumbered them, because they were on their own ground, and because European techniques, such as firearms, were less highly developed than they were later to become. However, their inability to unite effectively, or even to form lasting alliances, prevented them from achieving any decisive successes before the balance of numbers swung in favor of the colonists. In any case, no nomadic or seminomadic, sparsely scattered, hunting people, such as both Indians and aborigines were, has been able to stand against the expansion of Europe; and the North American Indians were peculiarly vulnerable geographically. They were able to wage a fine series of delaying actions, by adopting and perfecting the use of European weapons such as the musket and rifle, and above all the horse (a thing which the aborigines in their native state showed no ability or inclination to do), and they were even

23

able to teach the newcomers many things of use to them in the first stages of their struggle with nature,[12] such as the technique of hunting and of cultivating "the yellow, life-giving corn";[13] but, in the end, which was not long delayed, they, and to an even greater degree the aborigines, were at the invaders' mercy.

And there was not much of that. In both lands, the central government showed some sense of responsibility toward the natives and made some effort to temper the severity of the process which was described by one Australian Governor, in a triumph of euphemism, as "the natural progress of the aboriginal race towards extinction."[14] The record of the British imperial government was better in this respect than that of either the United States or the Australian government before the twentieth century, in some degree because of the pressure of the rising humanitarian movement in Britain, but mostly, it must be confessed, because it is much easier for those remote from such scenes of violent action to take lofty and enlightened views. The efforts it did make, such as those to try and control the movement of the two populations inland, were singularly ineffective;[15] just as abortive were efforts of the same kind made in New Zealand and South Africa. Only in Canada, according to the historian of the subject,[16] was the record of government notably better, partly as a result of the fur-trading tradition of Montreal, in which mode of exploiting the continent, almost alone among many, the friendship of the Indians was necessary; for its success private and exclusive possession of land was not indispensable, or even useful. It was the clamant demand of the whites for land which was the fundamental cause of the frontier's desire to be rid of the native; in the frontier's economic life, land is the prime essential, and it must be admitted that mankind has certainly and greatly benefited from the better use to which the European was able to put it.

If the record of the Canadian government was the best in the English-speaking world in its alleviation of the cruelties wrought by the frontiersmen upon the natives, it is perhaps not

unfair to say that that of the United States was the worst. Here
the latter paid the penalty of immediate democracy, for it
was less easy for the federal, let alone state, authorities to re-
sist the popular pressures of those on the spot, who adhered
to the view that the only good Indian was a dead one, than it
was for British governments with their aristocratic, authoritarian flavor. It is fair to observe, however, that for Americans
the problem was a larger one, with the result that their sins
were also larger. The formalities of making and breaking
treaties with the Indians, of erecting and destroying "permanent
barriers," and of giving and taking away reservations in each
successive generation, were not feasible or necessary in Australia,[17] though in a number of cases the consent of the blacks
to the appropriating of their lands was obtained by similar
methods. But if the United States erred greatly, she made rep-
aration (in so far as she had the power) on a handsome scale
in the end by the great change of opinion toward the Indians
which may be said to have begun with the Dawes Act of 1887:
the efforts of no other nation have really matched those of the
New Deal to rehabilitate the Indian, though Australia since
World War II has made rapid strides.[18]

Apart from government, only one agency perhaps has been
able effectively to temper the impact of Western civilization
upon native peoples—the missions. The Spaniards and the
French in America were the great missionaries, and it must be
said that missions were not so active on the United States
frontier until its day was done. Nor did Australia benefit much,
as did Africa and New Zealand, from the great British missionary movement of the nineteenth century, although the churches
did try to do something to prevent violence and exploitation;
the aborigines were usually thought too distant, too few, and
too primitive for attention, though at the present day the missions as well as the anthropologists are active. Thus, in the
early years, the Reverend Samuel Marsden departed from Australia and its children of nature in order to lead the first of the

great missions to the Maoris, whose souls were deemed much worthier of salvation.

However, in both Australia and the United States, as well as in Canada and New Zealand, the whole impact of the frontier upon the original inhabitants conformed remarkably to the same pattern. It is indeed one of the most striking examples there is of the similar reaction of the frontiers in similar circumstances. In both cases, partly from fear, but mostly from the passion for land, the newcomers were led into violence and ruthlessness; so much so, indeed, that it seems clear that humanitarian sentiments were simply unable to prevail until the frontiers were virtually closed, that is to say until it was plainly too late for them to be of any use. White diseases, white liquor, white removal of their means of livelihood, and violence or war in which the whites shared produced a catastrophic numerical decline among the natives which proceeded to near-extinction; the only effective protection was isolation or the discovery of an economic use for native labor, such as Australian cattle work. At this nadir, in both cases, whether due to native adjustment or a change of white attitudes, the decimation stopped and recovery began; this affected both Indians and aborigines, and occurred most rapidly, it is to be noted, among the mixed bloods.

One could not wish for a clearer instance than this clash of peoples of the analogy between the two frontiers; but when we turn from the frontiersmen and their native opponents to the way in which the former gained their livelihood, other comparisons which are quite as illuminating can be found.

3: *Products*

ITS ECONOMIC LIFE is at the core of the frontier concept. The existence of free land is the backbone of the thesis expounded by Turner, who was, indeed, in a measure an American manifestation of the tendency of late nineteenth-century historians and thinkers to concentrate their attention in the interpretation of men's actions upon their economic needs and desires and upon the powerful effect of their environment on those actions. It was perhaps his—and even possibly America's—special contribution to historical thought to emphasize the profound modifications which geography can make in the development of nations. He was not a narrowly economic, but rather a physiographical, determinist. Yet we err if we forget that economic environment occupied a primary place in his thought, and it is salutary that a fresh and penetrating mind, coming to the frontier thesis through the medium of British colonial history, should remind people that this is the case. Hancock has written: "In books dealing with European history, the frontier is something fixed. It is the sharp edge of a sovereign State. In books dealing with American history, the frontier is something moving. It is the advancing fringe of a dynamic society.[1] The European frontier is fundamentally a political thing. The American frontier is primarily an economic thing."[2]

But so manifold are the modes of economic life on the frontier that we must confine ourselves to a brief consideration of those points at which, so to speak, the frontiers of Australia and the United States touch. The basis of both in certain places and periods was subsistence agriculture. There were Starving Times at Port Jackson as well as at Jamestown, and men had for a space to be driven to dig and to sow. But it is not uncharacteristic of the two countries that were to be, that what

27

was done in the one by the Royal Governors (all the first three of whom were naval officers, straight from the quarter-deck) was in the other done by John Smith, a captain of a different kind, thrown up naturally by circumstances. Neither is it out of character that, arising from the fact of penal colonization, communal agricultural methods under government supervision were continued, though on an ever-diminishing scale, for over twenty years in Australia before they were finally and wholly displaced by individual enterprise, nor that this fact, combined with the difficulties of agriculture in the soil and climate of Port Jackson, kept the colonists long dependent upon imports of food, issued for the most part in the form of government rations.

This difference was not due merely to the relative richness of the American environment, but to the strangeness of the Australian; for, although America was a novel land, its east coast was in a sense a continuation of the forested environment of Western Europe, to which the settlers and their forebears had long been accustomed; as the poet puts it, although "the strange country" evoked a "childish wonderment," the first reaction after the long sea voyage was to be "light at heart . . ."

> Oh, the fair meadows, the goodly trees and tall,
> The fresh streams running in silver through the woods!
> 'Twas a land, a land![3]

How different must have been the reaction of the first Australians, whether prisoners or guards! How different, too, was their feeling about the continent even after they had seen a little of it.[4] In a famous passage the English Romantic novelist Marcus Clarke wrote: "In Australia alone is to be found the Grotesque, the Weird, the strange scribblings of Nature learning how to write. Some see no beauty in our trees without shade, our flowers without perfume, our birds who cannot fly, and our beasts who have not yet learned to walk on all fours."[5] Much more recent visitors from the mother country have felt the strangeness of the deep, liquid notes of the Australian magpie and the never-to-be-forgotten laughter of the kookaburra.[6] These feelings in the first settlers were analogous to their more practical difficulties in adjusting their way of life to the unfamiliar environment of the Australian Bush. Even to do the things that they could do at home, new methods and fresh ideas were necessary, and this was particularly true of food growing,[7] so that for this reason among others the efforts of governors, such as Bligh, to encourage the development of a class of small yeomen, or peasant farmers, were very slow in producing results.

In due course, however, subsistence agriculture must give way, at least in part, to production of a surplus for sale. By 1850 both Van Diemen's Land and also South Australia had a surplus of grain; intercolonial transport of it was easy enough by sea, but the difficulty, compared with America, was to get the crops to the seaboard. Even in the United States, where intercolonial maritime trade was equally easy, and internal communication much easier because of far better river transportation, this was an obstacle to the development of grain crops for sale as such. But in time they did develop; South Australia was exporting wheat to Britain by 1866, and the American colonies had from the earliest years much readier markets in the West Indies for their products. By the time of the steamship and the locomotive, the United States, because of its larger population and the greater area and productivity of its arable lands, was able to become the world's greatest exporter of grain up to that time.

One of the best methods of reaching a market for grain is, of course, to turn it into alcohol, and whisky early became a staple product of the American frontier which made agricultural surpluses manageable. In New England, rum was produced on an equally large scale from the molasses of the West Indies, and by the end of the eighteenth century the arm of her commerce was so long that probably the chief early sources of Australian rum were American ships. It was still the staple liquor of colonial America (giving place to whisky as the frontier moved away from the seaboard), but to an even greater degree was it that of Australia, where whisky occupied a very minor place.[8] Of course, the profitability of distillation did not escape the eye of government, and the evasion of excise by the production of "moonshine," or illicit grog, was long a common pursuit on both frontiers. The clash with government on this issue could be serious, as in the Whisky Rebellion during Washington's second administration; and, though the revolts are not comparable in most respects, the Rum Rebellion which overthrew "Bounty Bligh" a few years later in distant Australia was not by any means unconnected, as its name implies, with governmental restrictions on the import of rum.

For most of Australia's alcohol at first was imported, which reminds us—in the unlikely event of our forgetting it—that alcohol does not owe its importance in human affairs primarily to its transportability. In no sort of geographical area is its power of alleviating the distresses of life more welcome or more potent than on the frontier, where the tribulations of men are harsher and more numerous than in most other places. The American frontier knew how to put it to work, and it had as catastrophic effects on the Indians as it was to have on the aborigines of the antipodes; nor were American frontiersmen themselves unaddicted to the bottle. But the extent of the grip of alcohol upon the American West was mild compared with that upon the Australian colonies, beginning as they did in the squalor and misery of penal settlements.

From the first, rum bulked large in the many barter transactions of New South Wales; wages were often paid in it, and indeed were not infrequently unacceptable in any other form. Consumption was enormous; between September, 1800, and October, 1802, importation was on such a scale that there was enough for an annual rate of consumption of five gallons and three quarts of rum (to say nothing of two gallons and three quarts of wine) for each man, woman, and child in the colony. The habit was hard to break; one realistic novelist later wrote,[9] "The man who did not drink was as rare as the one without whiskers. Not sobriety so much as whether a man could carry liquor was the standard."[10] In the lore of the Far West among the cattlemen "blowing your pay," principally on drink, was a common enough phenomenon, but it did not assume the proportions of the universal, as did that of "drinking," or "knocking down," "your cheque" in the pastoral legend of the Bush; there was something almost dedicated about the routine of handing the contents of your pockets to the barkeeper on arrival after being paid and drinking it away and yourself into repeated insensibility until your penniless departure—and return next payday.

But whether as a native bribe, as a means of softening the hard realities of life, or as a method of transporting an agricultural surplus, Dante's *divino liquore* is closely interwoven with the history of the Australian and American frontiers.

The frontier, however, seldom waited for subsistence agriculture to develop a grain surplus. More often it sought in a more direct fashion that first essential for rapid growth, a cash crop—in the first place as a supplement to, but often later as a substitute for, grain. Such crops may be of many kinds; sometimes they are derived, as was pre-eminently the case with the American New England, not from the land but from the sea, in the form of fish.

In contrast with the Americans of the North, the Australians, even though they have remained a coastal people, have developed no great fisheries. This is partly because, relatively speaking, edible fish do not abound in their warm seas, but also because there was not a large ready market for Australian fish (as there was for American, in the South, the West

Indies, and Europe), for distance, and above all the Tropics, were an almost insuperable barrier. Nor was Australia, except perhaps in some degree for Tasmania, nearly as well equipped with timber suitable for the construction of large vessels as was North America.

But such natural difficulties, even when added to colonial or frontier lack of capital, do not fully explain the comparative dearth of Australian maritime enterprise, for in whaling, and to a lesser degree, sealing, Australia had great natural advantages as a base in the Southern Hemisphere. And, indeed, whaling flourished in Australian waters in the nineteenth century, but in the hands of Americans rather than Australians. It is true that until 1813 the growth of Australian whaling was hampered by the monopoly of the East India Company, and by English duties on the import of whale products, but that superior American energy and enterprise, in "this most perilous mode of hardy industry"[11] which Burke observed and lauded in such matchless language, must count for much. As the historian of the subject writes, given the enormous disparities of distance "it is difficult to find any adequate reasons for American success in outstripping their colonial and British rivals other than the greater initiative which they displayed."[12] This was not so easy to develop in the authoritarian atmosphere of a prison community, any more than it proved to be in the slave South. This appears to be one of the fields in which the hustling individualism of the North gained it decisive preeminence.

But the land in America had crops to offer as rewarding as those of the ocean, for a number of years without any greater need of cultivation. High in importance among these came furs, which were the foundation of Canadian development. Owing to their transportability and the demand for them, they were, from the beginning, an important element in the growth of the American colonies. A virtually universal activity on the frontier of the timbered lands of the East and later of the forested areas of the Far West, and especially the Northwest, the fur trade particularly flourished in early years in New York, with its easy access to the trans-Appalachian region through the Hudson-Mohawk Valley. But no such development was possible in Australia, which was very poor in animals having fur of any value, while even trade in cattle hides, of which it could produce many, was slow to develop, although British merchants were able to maintain such trade with equally distant California in the years before it became part of the United States.

Australia was somewhat better endowed with another ready-made crop, timber, but even here her resources were of a restricted kind, for while she has reasonable supplies of excellent hardwoods, she lacks softwoods, which are in most demand for everyday purposes, such as housing. The United States, on the other hand, abounds in good soft timbers.[13] This meant, too, that Australians were not able in the first half of the nineteenth century to take advantage of the still flourishing market for naval stores. And even in hardwoods she is not quite as well off as might appear, for the Australian climate in most places twists and warps beyond utility a much higher proportion of even the good timber than is the normal habit of nature.[14]

But the greatest economic resources of the two lands in the days when their frontiers were actively growing were the specialized agricultural harvests of particular areas, the so-called staple crops. In the development of the frontiers these crops were of vital importance.

The first of these in America, the mainland prototype, was tobacco, by the production of which Jamestown grew to Virginia; it was the first great staple of the colonial South. Others came later, such as rice in South Carolina by the beginning of the eighteenth century, but it was not a product which affected the frontier, since it was confined to highly specialized geographical areas. The same was also true of the sugar industry, centering in Louisiana, which did not begin to flourish until the nineteenth century. The natural pace of frontier expansion in the case of tobacco, as in that of cotton later, was accelerated by the rapidity with which persistent cultivation of this single crop exhausted the soil, thus forcing owners to move on to new lands. This was a contributory cause of the fact that the South led the Westward Movement until well into the nineteenth century.

The most characteristic mode of tobacco culture was the plantation. These large agricultural units, cultivated by slave labor, were in fact a means of combining the advantages of the colony of *"peuplement"* with those of the colony of *"exploitation."* But the plantation system had its most characteristic and important manifestation in the culture of cotton, the greatest of the staple crops, intimately connected not only with the onset of the American Civil War but with the economic development of Britain and indeed of Western civilization. It was of decisive consequence in the development of the frontier. Confined at first to the coast by the fact that Sea Island cotton, whose long staple alone made it worth while, would not grow elsewhere, the invention of the cotton gin in 1792 made possible the economic cultivation of the short-staple variety which would grow inland, and this threw open vast tracts of the United States to profitable development. The exploitation by cotton planters of the great Black Belt of Alabama, Mississippi, Louisiana, Arkansas, and Texas, one of the most fertile areas of soil in the world, was the most important single economic fact in the history of the United States, and perhaps even of mankind, for the next fifty years.

Australia, on the other hand, was slow in developing the great agricultural staples, and she never became to a considerable extent dependent upon any of them. There was an abortive effort to grow cotton when the Civil War provided an exceptional market, but it collapsed altogether as soon as the South began to compete again. This was the result partly of the old familiar trinity of Australian disadvantages—climate, soil, and distance —but to these was added the difficulty of labor shortage. The most interesting Australian development was that of sugar, whose production in the United States is, owing to climatic conditions, geographically very limited. Yet for comparative purposes the growth of the Queensland sugar industry is of absorbing interest.

The well-watered and long, though narrow, coastal plain of northern New South Wales and Queensland is ideally suited to sugar cane, and its broad rivers provide good access to the near-by coast. Queensland was very much a frontier area in the 1860's when pastoral expansion was renewed after the check administered by the gold rushes of the previous decade and promoted by the operation of free selection laws in the southern states: "scores of southern squatters sought safety there from the free selector. Black spearsmen . . . besieged . . . numerous station households in a strength and determination forgotten farther south . . . But native resistance could not stop the invaders . . . But climatically the north was less suitable for sheep than were the western plains of New South Wales."[15] This gave an added incentive for the development of the peculiar agricultural possibilities of the coastal strip.

The sporadic cultivation of sugar on the coast had long been known, but by the 1870's it really got into its stride, so that in 1872-73 some 65 mills turned out 6,000 tons of sugar and 160,000 gallons of rum, which met the needs of the colony and left a surplus of £37,000 worth to be exported. The temporary cotton culture of the previous decade had brought the first substantial importation of Polynesian, or Kanaka, labor, and now "blackbirding," a process often not very far removed from slave trading, began on a considerable scale. In all, about 47,000 islanders were brought to Queensland as sugar boomed, so that in 1880 £280,000 worth of sugar was exported. But the importation of colored labor aroused vigorous opposition not only in the southern parts of Queensland and the rest of Australia, but also in the mother country, whose humanitarian movements were powerful as well as sensitive, not only to dangers so recently exemplified in the Civil War but also to the fact that Polynesian mortality in Australia was four times the European.

As long as Queensland remained a separate colony, the planters of the north fought a bitter and successful battle to retain colored labor: "They forged, in the North Queensland Separation Movement, a weapon which (like the Confederate States of Jefferson Davis) gave their purpose the guise of a crusade for self-determination."[16] Partly owing to a brilliant delaying action by Samuel Griffith, premier of Queensland and adamantine in his opposition to colored labor (the favorite toast of the planters was "D.S.G.," for "Damn Sam Griffith"), and partly to the opposition of Britain, secession was prevented (despite sound geographical arguments in its favor and an actual vote for division of the colony in the Queensland legislature in 1897) until the time when Queensland as a whole was merged in the Commonwealth of Australia in 1901. Then the cause of the north Queenslanders was lost in face of the resolute White Australia policy supported by the vast majority of Australians. For its success they were prepared to pay—and it is not easy to think that they were wrong—a high economic price; the sugar industry of the Australian Tropics was enabled to develop as a white labor enterprise, through the encouragement of small-scale agricultural and refining units by a very substantial government subsidy. But it was a close call: as Shann writes, "the Australian communities, festooned along a coast-line of ten thousand miles, are nowadays strangely uniform in social structure", but "Queensland once promised to evolve quite a different social tissue comparable to the planter-aristocracy of the Old Dominion and the Carolinas in the days of Calhoun . . ."[17]

36

But fascinating as is this potential analogy, there is an actual comparison with cotton cultivation which is even more compelling. This is not with an agricultural staple at all, but with a pastoral one, the living harvest of the sheep. The difference is, as the phrase "wool-farming" illustrates, in one sense a small one; as the United States, to some extent, grew to economic strength through cotton, so, though to a much greater degree, Australia was carried to wealth on the sheep's back. From the first, one or two of the free settlers in Australia realized the need for a staple export: outstanding among them was one of the officers of the first garrison, John Macarthur, a stormy petrel in Australia's embryonic politics, but a man of vision and resolution who saw that wool would be the foundation of Australia's economy. He perceived that good sheep, cheap convict labor, and empty convict transports homeward bound[18] provided the key, and he soon imported Merino sheep and began to improve his breed. No other attempts were comparable to his, and for the most part the breeds remained very poor, while efforts to turn hemp, flax, timber, and even coal into cash crops failed. Certainly, original auspices for the sheep were not favorable; in September, 1788, Governor Phillip wrote: "One sheep only remains of upwards of seventy which I purchased at the Cape of Good Hope. It is the rank grass under the trees that has destroyed then . . ."[19] It is now known that sheep do much better on the dry western slopes of the mountains than on the coast, although Macarthur wrote even of it in 1805, there are "tracts of land adapted for pastures so boundless that no assignable limits can be set to the number of fine-woolled sheep which can be raised . . ."[20]

Thus, by 1813 there were still only about 50,000 sheep in Australia, and of these Macarthur's almost alone were a pure, tough, thriving breed produced primarily for wool; the remainder were indifferent animals bred equally for meat and wool. By 1821, the first year of commercial export, though estimates vary considerably, it seems probable that there were well over 200,000 sheep; after this Macarthur's views were fully vindicated, for in New South Wales there were one million by 1832, and thirteen million by 1849, producing excellent "clips" of magnificent wool. By 1860 in Australia as a whole there were 20 million, and by 1890 there was attained a peak, not quite reached again for thirty years, of 100 million.[21] This development of wool through seventy years, 1820-90, is worthy to be matched with that of cotton in America between 1790 and 1860.

But before a detailed comparison is made, it must be observed that the United States itself has grown wool on a considerable scale, and that in certain American areas there have been resemblances to the Australian pastoral industry. The so-called "sheep-craze," which swept New England between 1825 and 1840, was followed by another in Ohio in the 1840's. But the chief pastoral resemblance is in the West, where conditions are similar to those in Australia, and where most of America's sheep are raised at the present day. The sheep men, migrating from the Ohio Valley in the 1870's, moved into California and the southern Rockies and then in the 1880's invaded the Great Plains. Unlike the Australian squatters they had, for the most part, to struggle for their land—often with some shedding of human and much of ovine blood—with cattlemen who had preceded them, but in suitable areas they were able to win out, for "no force could hold back such a profitable enterprise . . ."[22] But their numbers never equaled those of Australia, which in 1938-39 had 111 million sheep to America's 51 million and in 1949-50 112 million to her 30 million. It is almost indisputable that no primary economic enterprise in the United States has ever matched in significance for the whole economy the importance of wool in Australian economic development, but cotton probably came nearer to doing so than any other.

The cotton and wool systems were comparable in many respects. The cotton plantation and the pastoral lease—even allowing for the fact that in both cases the large unit came to be thought of as typical, although it was not—both needed to be of greater extent than the holding of the wheat or corn farmer. Whereas a farmer might be content with 160 acres in a good area of the North, and perhaps double that in a good Australian agricultural locality, a middle-sized cotton plantation might be between 400 and 1,000 acres and a large one about two or three thousand, while a pastoral lease might run to almost any size over 2,000 acres. Cotton required less land than wool, but both needed less than cattle; only in the arid West did the farmer essentially need as much as the smallest cotton planter of the South. Of course, whereas cotton land needs to be both wet and fertile, sheep will graze well on arid and not very thickly vegetated land, though the rapid exhaustion of soil under excessive cotton cultivation can match the effects of the overstocking of sheep runs.

For both, though much more particularly for cotton, cheap labor was essential, and was supplied by Negro slaves in the one case and convicts or exconvicts in the other. The two were admirably fitted for their roles; the slaves could be controlled closely in their gangs on intensive cotton cultivation, and the "lags," or more particularly the "old lags," could be left to their task of sheepherding amid the dismal isolation of the Bush, in which they could only survive in some such fashion. It is a commonplace that the simplicity of the work made cotton an ideal slave crop, and Shann writes of sheep tending, "The routine work was within the competence even of convicts."[23] The vast majority of shepherds and hutkeepers were "old hands," and "Station employment was . . . in the early days primarily a backwater of the tragic stream of transportation."[24] It is not too much to claim that the pastoral system of Australia in the first half of the nineteenth century was as much built on the basis of the convict, as was the plantation system of America in the same period on the foundation of the slave. For both industries, by historical chance and the action of the British people and government, a bountiful supply of such labor, which could be exploited ruthlessly without much external restraint, had been available at just the time when it was needed.

Both also required large capital resources, though men could for a time on the frontier itself grow to wealth by expanding their own initially limited activities. Capital was needed not only for the purchase of land and supplies, but also for that of slaves on the one hand and sheep on the other. Both relied for their solvency on an international, largely British, commodity market over which they had little or no control, and because of the steadily rising price of slaves (who did not increase naturally as swiftly as sheep) it seems probable that the financial difficulties of the planter were the more severe. But both were to a great degree dependent upon the British capitalist; both were, indeed, excellent examples of the indebtedness of frontier areas, for the cotton planters were perennially in debt, often to British houses, and the squatters were even more tied to the London money market. It has been argued that the Cotton South was approaching an economic crisis of the first magnitude when the Civil War began, owing to overinvestment in land and slaves, and in the second half of the nineteenth century there was an increasing tendency for the pastoral companies, with their greater financial resources, to replace many individual squatters who had overstretched themselves financially.[25] This availability of British capital was of the greatest importance in the development of both the cotton and wool frontiers, and of almost equal consequence was the remarkably similar part played by British houses, in the initial stage, in marketing and transporting the annual crops. The two processes, of course, were interdependent; it was the flow of exported raw material which made possible the importation of capital.

The analogy here is shown by some of the figures. Wool began in the 1830's to grow with astonishing rapidity and soon became by far Australia's biggest export; the proportion it constituted of her exports was drastically reduced in the fifties by the gold discoveries, but in 1861 it was still 22 percent, and by 1890 had risen again to 33 percent.[26] In 1860 cotton constituted two thirds of the total value of United States exports. The importance of the British connection is illustrated by the fact that Great Britain took virtually all the wool crop for many years and roughly half of the cotton crop, while in 1850 half of Britain's wool imports came from Australia and about four fifths of its cotton imports from the United States. But the most striking figures are the leaping over-all ones. They are approximately as follows. Cotton production in the United States was: 1820, 160 million lbs.; 1850, 1,000 million lbs.; 1860, 2,300 million lbs. Wool exports from Australia—and it exported almost all its crop—were: 1830, 2 million lbs.; 1840, 10 million lbs.; 1849, 35 million lbs. By 1891 the total Australian clip was 641 million lbs. This remarkable progression reflects another side of the relationship of the two frontiers with the then economic center of the Western world, Great Britain; both were great consumers of its manufactured goods.

From the beginning, the Australian market has always been, and still is, dominated by British manufactured goods; at first this was enforced by the protectionist system centering on the Navigation Acts. However, when these were repealed, and at about the same time Australia's colonies began to attain self-government, the dependence upon Britain lessened only gradually. Victoria, a small state in area, led the way to protection, but New South Wales, the largest pastoral state, retained free trade until the coming of federation and the protectionist policy of the Commonwealth government. Even now, for example, Australia has only just begun to produce its own automobiles, and throughout the nineteenth century it was absolutely dependent upon British manufactures. This dependence is very similar to that of the South upon British and Yankee industry in the ante-bellum period; the cotton-producing states not only needed to trade with their best customer, but could get their imports more cheaply from efficient British industry than from anywhere else. Thus, they were, for the most part, free traders, and, during the years when they were powerful in the national government there occurred—between 1832 and 1857—the only really steady progress in the reduction of tariffs which took place in American history before the 1930's. This domination of the American market by British industrial products, though not as complete as in Australia, was notable. Thus, in the early years of independence about one third of all America's imports were British; between 1821 and 1850 the figure was around 40 percent; between 1855 and 1859 the proportion seems to have sunk to about a third once more; and by the years 1885-89 and 1905-08 a steady decline had reduced it to roughly one fifth and one tenth, respectively. It was in the second quarter of the century that Britain's exports to the United States were most important both in its own economy and that of the United States,[27] and it was in the 1850's that the cotton exports of the United States were most important both to her and to Britain, while her total exports to Britain of all commodities were never more important to both than at this period.[28]

This illustrates clearly that intimate conjunction of the cotton and wool frontiers with British industry, which arose directly from the prodigious and unprecedented economic development of the Industrial Revolution. This great convulsion which seized upon Great Britain, little comprehended though it was by its contemporaries, made a reality for the first time of the unity of the world's economy which Adam Smith embodied in his potent phrase "the great mercantile republic."[29] It tied together, with seemingly unbreakable bonds, areas which are as remote from one another as are Lancashire and Yorkshire, for instance, from Dubbo and Dallas, or Longreach and Little Rock. What made this possible was the insatiable and increasing demand of the British textile industries for raw materials, and their equally huge supply of finished products. The Australian and American frontiers were particularly tied to Britain; the 6,000-acre farm, the mean of South African development, was akin in size to the units of cotton and wool production, but it was never linked in this intimate way to British industry, because it was much more self-sufficient and never came to depend in the same fashion upon the cultivation of a great staple crop. This Anglo-American and Anglo-Australian connection underlines that element of chance which can appear in the greatest economic movements, the chance that there existed at just the right moment for British industrial development (and thus for the economic progress of all mankind) great tracts of suitable land, under suitable governments and suitable conditions of capital and labor supply, for the unparalleled growth of two basic human commodities. The singular, swift, and simultaneous exploitation of the great Black Belt of the South and the vast outback of New South Wales, each consisting of some 250,000 square miles of virgin land, is a unique phenomenon, and in the years 1820-60 the likeness between them is close. It is, indeed, in reality the only period when there is a sense in Australian frontier history of something akin to the resistless surge of the American Westward Movement; the only time of which it could be written

> The mountains saw them marching by;
> They faced the all-consuming drought,
> They could not rest in settled land,
> Their faces ever westward bent
> Beyond the farthest settlement,
> Responding to the challenge cry
> Of "better country farther out."[30]

But in both cases the peculiar society produced by the cultivation of cotton and wool on lands made available by the moving frontier was to have a swift end. It was not that the lands ran out (though the sentiments of the cotton planter and the squatter, as, at about the same time, they faced the Great American Desert and the "dead heart" of Australia, must have been very much alike), nor was it that the lands ceased to be on the frontier. It was that the social system, based on the possession of capital and the availability of cheap servile or semiservile labor, in which in some respects they shared, could not stand against the political and social forces of democracy and the economic force of industrialism. Yet, in their brief day, squattocracy and slavocracy had much in common. The prosperous latter-day squatters, modeling themselves on the Macarthurs at Camden Park, were described by Henry Parkes as "the old colonial magnates, who hitherto had ruled with a peculiar order of absolutism representing the artificial feeling of domination on the one hand and of submission on the other which characterized old Virginian society."[31] Upon the fleeting basis of a passing economic ascendancy they endeavored to build an aristocratic social system,[32] which looked to the English past for its inspiration, but which lacked the long breeding of the nobility of the mother country; these squatters were somewhat more ephemeral than the planters, but few even of the latter could avoid the excesses of a *nouveau riche* class modeling themselves on an aristocracy of which they are not a part. In both, the idolum was largely illusion; that of the South was to the poet a "purple dream";[33] that of the pastoralists was to the historian a "dream of a colonial gentry . . . leading the colonies in politics as in wealth and culture. It was an idea already tottering in the England of the Great Exhibition of 1851; but the pedigree . . . is to be found in . . . the age of Burke . . ."[34] Yet, while it lasted—longer again in the case of the South—their power was a reality, and they fought hard to retain it; the squatters had hardly seized it in the political sphere in Australia before it was wrested from them by a triumphant democracy (though they retained their economic influence much longer), but it needed a vast civil conflict to destroy the much greater and more firmly entrenched power of the planter aristocracy. Both were vulnerable, though the planters more so, to the humanitarian movements radiating from Britain, which resulted in the abolition of both transportation and slavery: ultimately, though, they were even more at the mercy of industrialism. It is indeed ironical that these rural patriarchal systems, "the pastoral rebellion of the earth against machines, against the Age of Steam,"[35] should in the end have been overthrown by the impact of that very industrialism which their distant frontiers had nurtured and fed to greatness.

It was not only in a metaphorical sense that the frontiers fed the great cities, and, whereas the Australian sheep (unlike that of New Zealand) has been primarily a wool-producing animal, horned-cattle raising in both Australia and America has been primarily directed to the provision of food rather than hides. Both frontiers have always had large areas suitable for free grazing, but the full development of the cattle industry did not come in either country until steam, canning, and refrigeration in turn increased the practicability of transporting meat to great urban areas. There was, through lack of a comparable market or comparable transportation facilities at the end of the trail, nothing in Australian history to match the era of the "Long Drive" from southern Texas nearly a thousand miles to the north, though herds are driven great distances in Queensland, Western Australia, and the Northern Territory. Indeed, the development of the Australian cattle industry has, in all but the very recent past, been in some respects disappointing, even making due allowance for geographical difficulties. The Australian character has had a say in this as well as the Australian environment. The Northern Territory is the salient example, for, given the way in which cattle now flourish in central Australia, and given the amount of capital which the great British firm of Vestey's, for instance, were willing to sink in the meat industry there between 1910 and 1919, it is surprising that more has not been accomplished. But labor troubles made the position impossible at Darwin, and in the latter year Vestey's closed down altogether, leaving the huge hulk of a deserted, rusting, and rotting factory as a kind of mausoleum for many years of Australian hope. Of a project for a port in the Northern Territory, a one-time governor wrote: "If a similar plan had been drawn up for a port in the United States it would have been carried out. America's development has been built up on enterprises of this kind. In some way, however, Australia and its Governments appear to lack the driving force that is so necessary if every portion of this great continent is to be developed."[36]

But the Northern Territory is, under wise postwar administration, making renewed progress,[37] the cattle industry in particular flourishing as never before; and in any case Australia as a whole cannot be judged by the Territory, whose career is not only checkered and highly controversial, but whose boundaries in 1951 contained only 7 percent of the cattle of Australia (though 10 percent of her beef cattle). But it is from our point of view an area of great interest, because it is "Australia's Frontier Province"; with the exception of Alaska it is the last Australian or American frontier.[38] The visitor to the land is at once and forcibly reminded of the analogy between the two cattle frontiers in past and present, for he sees again, in modified form, the cattle lands of the West. The aboriginal stockman bizarrely affects (or, it would be as true to say, finds convenient) the garb of the cowboy; the land abounds in water-raising windmills and is crossed by numerous stock routes with their natural or artificial waterholes; men live upon horseback and handle the great herds in much the same way as their American counterparts;[39] and there are holdings (matching those of, for example, Texas) of 1,000 square miles in extent. The historian, too, is conscious of the similarities, as for instance in the effects of drought and overstocking; thus, the years of subnormal rainfall in Australia between 1895 and the drought year 1902, following on the seductively wet years from 1889 to 1894, produced very similar results to the drought of 1886 in the American West, which followed a period of good conditions but was sandwiched between two bitterly cold winters. The deaths of vast numbers of stock under horrible conditions not only left its mark upon the minds of those who saw them, but had economic repercussions of a serious kind as far away as Britain. In the State of Wyoming the number of cattle sank from 9 million in 1886 to 3 million in 1895: in the State of Queensland from 7 million in 1894 to 2½ million in 1902. In both cases the results were similar; a greater caution in the extension of pastoral holdings; a greater caution on the part of investors; and a tendency toward smaller and more effectively enclosed ranches and stations, in which the land was more fully utilized and treated with more respect.

4: Land

ALL THE WAYS by which the frontier lives, except those of the sea, directly depend upon the good earth,[1] even furs and timber, which have to be cultivated like other crops once the frontier has passed. Land is the kernel of the frontier problem. C. J. Rowe wrote in 1883, "In young colonies the land is everything."[2] But, as Hancock has noted,[3] appreciation of this fact is as least as old as Adam Smith, and in a sense it was the application of the idea to the history of the United States which was the most important contribution of Turner:[4] "The most significant thing about the American frontier is, that it lies at the hither edge of free land."[5] The development of systems of tenure and ownership of land is crucial in a comparative study of frontiers, and provides us with many interesting analogies. It is, however, essential to realize that the direct influence of the United States upon Australia in this matter was very important; at one of the most crucial periods in Australian land history, the years immediately following the granting of self-government in the mid-nineteenth century, the American example was widely known in Australia, partly owing to the great influx of population in the gold rush, some of whom knew the United States. By 1851 in America the Pre-emption system had operated fully for a decade and the Homestead agitation was well under way, so that there can be little doubt that the Australian clamor for closer settlement which burst forth at that time owed much to the American experience.

Despite the greater diversity of the American environment, the history of its land policies is somewhat the simpler of the two, for after 1787, in effect, the whole public domain of the United States was in the hands of the federal government.[6] The public domain of Australia was at first in the hands of the imperial authorities, but even so there was no real uniformity of policy between colonies until the very eve of the granting of self-government, after which the individual states effectually controlled their own lands and adopted different land policies. Even after federation in 1901 the lands continued to be owned and administered by the states, except for the Northern and Capital Territories. The development of land legislation did, however, follow something of the same pattern in all the states except South Australia.

Hamilton's belief that the lands of the federal government should be a great financial resource was closely paralleled by the view of the Imperial government, expressed by Earl Grey: "These lands constitute a vast estate, which has been acquired . . . by the very large expense which has been incurred by the Mother-country in establishing, maintaining, and protecting its Colonies. This estate the Crown holds as trustee for the benefit of all its subjects . . ."[7] Hamilton's view was opposed by that of Jefferson, who saw the western lands (to which he so vastly added by the Louisiana Purchase) as the patrimony of the citizens of a great popular government, and who favored the easy acquisition of land. It is true that, in practice, there was not so much difference between them on this issue as on others, for Hamilton proposed in 1790 lots of a maximum of 100 acres at 30 cents an acre and Jefferson's advent to power brought no great changes in land policy,[8] but Hamilton's emphasis on the proceeds of sale produced a tendency among his Eastern successors to keep lots large enough and prices high enough to favor revenue, and very often the land speculator, whereas Jefferson's Western descendants desired ever cheaper land in ever smaller lots. American land policy between 1785 and 1862 can, very broadly, be seen as the slow triumph of the Jeffersonian point of view.

In Australia things were very different. Speaking generally, it would be true to say that in the nineteenth century the pastoralist, needing large tracts of grazing lands, asserted and retained his ascendancy nearly everywhere except South Australia (and to some extent Tasmania). This was not because the majority of Australians wished it, but because nature would have it so: the economic facts of American life in the years before the Civil War were in accord with the development of popular land legislation, but in Australia they did not lend themselves to it until the coming of modern agricultural knowledge and transportation methods at the end of the century. There intervened, therefore, in the middle years of the century, a curious period when Australian democracy was able to pass legislation aimed at smaller and cheaper agricultural holdings, but was unable to enforce it because of the economic advantages of the pastoralists, who enjoyed the support of that same law of nature which Daniel Webster declared rendered California and New Mexico impossible as a habitat for cotton slavery.

The story of Australian land settlement was further complicated by the influence of that strange but powerful theorist of colonization, Edward Gibbon Wakefield. He was very much aware of the American experience, but his ideas were more akin to those of Hamilton than to those of the American advocates of cheap land, for he believed that its price should be kept sufficiently high to ensure a proper supply of labor, which is reminiscent of Hamilton's view that immigration should be limited to the amount which can properly be absorbed by the economic system. His ideas had a particular appeal to the Imperial government because they seemed to provide an answer to the problem of surplus population at home, and they played a considerable part in the development of South Australia, which became the continent's most prosperous agricultural, wheat-producing area.[9] This was the first region of Australia in which relatively small farmers were able to succeed in the way that they were able to do in the whole Northeast and Middle West of the United States.

Nature had the last word in frontier development, however,

in the United States also. For when the Westward Movement reached the Great Plains and beyond, not only had the methods of settlement to be revolutionized, but the whole structure of federal land legislation was affected. Once again the similarity of the whole of this area to Australia is illustrated, for the long trend in America toward smaller maximum units of land, which culminated in the Homestead Act of 1862, was reversed when it became realized that small holdings were simply not economic in this area. This offered the same affront to the views of an individualist democracy, as did the hold of the pastoralists on the land in Australia. And although there was the same denunciation of the dubious means by which men acquired large tracts of land, the efforts to check such developments were just as unsuccessful. In both places the small man, armed with political power, found himself almost helpless in the face of a hostile nature, for a nature which supplies too little water is essentially hostile.

This democratic trend in American land legislation in the years before the Homestead Act is plain. The basic instrument, the Ordinance of 1785, adopted the fundamental land unit of the six-miles-square township, divided into thirty-six numbered "sections" of one square mile, or 640 acres. The minimum sale was to be of one section, at a price of not less than a dollar an acre, which effectively prevented pioneer farmers from purchasing, since they could not raise so large a sum as $640.[10] In the years of Federalist power the Act of 1796 made conditions even less liberal, by raising the minimum price to two dollars an acre (although with one-year credit for a dollar of it) and by retaining the provision that the auction sales could only take place in the East. But in 1800 the Republicans passed a measure which allowed generous credit, which opened local land offices in the West, and which reduced the minimum amount that could be purchased to 320 acres; thus, although the price of two dollars an acre was retained, the purchaser only needed to put down $160 in cash. In 1804 the minimum cash price was reduced to $1.64 per acre and the minimum amount that could be sold to 160 acres, while relief acts for those who could not complete their payments became frequent. However, when a financial crisis appeared in the years after the Treaty of Ghent, Congress passed the Act of 1820, which abolished credit payments, but lowered the minimum price to $1.25 and the minimum amount to 80 acres. Nevertheless, by 1832 eleven relief acts had been passed, which in effect restored a credit system.[11]

From this time attention shifted from the size of holdings to the method of acquiring them, though price still remained, as always, the primary consideration. Efforts to obtain the principle of graduation, or gradual reductions in the price of unsaleable land, failed, but the new surge of Western influence associated with Jacksonian Democracy produced the enactment of a system of pre-emption. So slow was Congress to arrange a survey and sale of Western lands, principally owing to the feeling in the East against too swift a development of them, that settlement far outran survey, so that in 1828, according to Robbins, something like two thirds of the population of Illinois were "squatting" on lands belonging to the United States government. Beginning in 1830 a number of Pre-emption Acts were passed by Congress which culminated in the Act of 1841; this allowed virtually any adult American male who was not disqualified by the possession of too much land elsewhere and who would fulfill certain conditions, to pre-empt 160 acres of public land at the government minimum price of $1.25 per acre. In effect, this incorporated in a permanent system the democratic right of a wide range of individuals to purchase public lands, to which they had staked a claim by genuine residence, at a reasonable price; this put the pioneer more nearly on a level with the speculator and virtually ended the idea that revenue was the paramount object of land sales. From this it was but a small step for the West, now conscious of its power, to demand free land; but largely owing to the opposition of the South, particularly in the Senate, it was not until 1862, after Secession, that the Homestead Act was passed. This assured to the same classes of persons as the Pre-emption Act of 1841 the right to enter a maximum of 160 acres of the surveyed public domain for a $10 fee designed to cover administrative costs. Title could be acquired by continuous residence and cultivation over five years, and a further fee of $26 (or $34 on the Pacific coast); the homestead right could be transmuted into full title by the payment of $1.25 per acre at any time after six months.

Thus, the process of reducing the minimum quantity and minimum price of public land, which had begun in 1800 and continued with periodically renewed energy under frontier pressure, was virtually complete. But at the time that the Homestead Act, opening up land to the small farmer, was passed, the line of occupation had reached, very roughly, the 98th meridian, with some settlement on the Pacific coast—in other words the Westward Movement had reached the arid lands of the West. This meant that the frontier passed, for the most part, out of the good agricultural land which had been the norm of American development at just the time when the public domain had finally been made as fully available as possible to the pioneer farmer. It is true that there was public domain left behind the frontier, but in general it was of steadily deteriorating quality, while the public domain to the west, for different reasons, was also inferior land. The effect upon land legislation was striking: it now began to keep land cheap, but to enlarge the maximum units which might be held. This reversed the democratic tendency of the previous three quarters of a century by favoring the big man, but now nature was clearly on his side. Whereas in the fertile lands hitherto opened up the problem had been the political one of getting land into small, and hence cheap, enough lots for the little man, who had no difficulty in making a very satisfactory living off 160, or even 80, acres, it now began to appear that the difficulty was the economic one of

making any living at all out of land with such a poor rainfall—
a task which was pretty nearly impossible on 320, let alone 160,
acres. Unless his land was irrigated, a farmer on the Great
Plains needed between 360 and 640 acres, and a rancher anything between 2,000 and 50,000 acres, according to the locality.
Evasions of the law, with larger holdings as their object, may
often have been the work of speculators, but without units of
increased acreage the West could not have been economically
settled.

None of the legislation which was passed frankly recognized
the need for larger units without special conditions, and so all
of it was to some degree the subject of fraud. The Timber
Culture Act of 1873, as modified in 1878, allowed a home-
steader to acquire a further quarter section if he put ten acres
of it to timber within a certain period. The Desert Land Act of
1877 allowed a settler in the West to purchase a whole section
of 640 acres, if he would irrigate it within three years, for a
down payment of 25 cents, the rest to follow within three years.
This was pre-eminently a cattleman's law and was much abused.
The Timber and Stone Act of 1878 authorized the sale of sur-
veyed lands, which were unfit for cultivation and valuable
chiefly for timber and stone, in quantities of not more than 160
acres for a minimum of $2.50 per acre. All these measures
gave great opportunities to land speculators, who were also able
to purchase direct from the government in huge quantities,
until an Act in 1889 limited sales to 320 acres; thus, between
1862 and 1889 more land was sold than in the years before
the Homestead Act. Between 1862 and the close of the century
speculators are estimated to have acquired about 100,000,000
acres, while homesteaders were granted 80,000,000 acres. Railroads and states also received princely grants, so that Billington
writes: "Half a billion acres were surrendered to monopolists
in an era when orators boasted the United States was giving
land free to its poverty-stricken masses! . . . Probably not more

than one acre in every nine went directly to small pioneers, the supposed beneficiaries of the Homestead Act!"[12]

The history of Australian land legislation [13] had some things in common with that of the United States, particularly in the second half of the nineteenth century, but there were great divergences in the early years, and the outcome of the Australian legislation was very different from that of the American except in the West. Until the abolition of free grants of land in all the Australian colonies in 1831, only a very small proportion of the land disposed of was sold. In that year a system of sale by auction at an "upset," or minimum, price of five shillings[14] per acre was instituted, and from that time on the imperial government was dominated by the Wakefieldian idea of maintaining a high price for land in order to subsidize emigration and provide labor in the colonies.[15] In other words, their policy was one dictated from the center of political power for economic reasons and not one formulated in accordance with the wishes of the men actually on the frontier, in which it resembled the early, Eastern-dominated land legislation of the United States Congress. In much the same way the next years (until the grant of self-government) saw a steady and increasingly successful economic and political struggle by the men on the ground, in this case chiefly the pastoralists, to gain control of the lands on the borders of settlement. Only this was an oligarchical interest, in a number of respects somewhat like that of the Cotton South, and different from the democratic interest of the North. The policy of the Imperial government did nothing to make land easy to get, for in 1838, by Colonial Office order, the upset price was raised to twelve shillings per acre, a principal reason being given as the desire to keep up the supply of labor by preventing laborers "from too quickly acquiring land by the saving of (their) high wages, and too readily gratifying the desire, inherent in all men, of independence."[16] Another reason, less pleasing to the pastoralists, was to prevent dispersion and confine the colonists to the settled districts; from 1829 the government endeavored, without success, to keep the taking up of new land within the so-called Nineteen Counties of coastal settlement around Sydney, but the aspiring pastoralists squatted on the land ever farther westward, and their political efforts were directed for the next eighteen years to acquiring some form of security of tenure for these occupied but unpurchased lands.

This goal was approached by stages, Acts of Council in 1833, 1834, and 1836, giving a limited recognition to squatting,[17] which proceeded apace, so that by 1840 there were about 5,000 free persons and nearly 3,000 assigned servants on some 700 stations in the outback. Meanwhile, after a brief and unsuccessful experiment in the abolition of auction and the sale of land at the high fixed price of twenty shillings outside the Nineteen Counties, the Australian Lands Act of the Imperial Parliament in 1842 raised the upset price of land in all colonies to twenty shillings per acre, where it remained for over twenty years, during the first half of which little was sold. But this was no help to the squatting pastoralists, who complained bitterly, as Governor Gipps wrote, "of being governed by a Secretary of State who does not know that three acres of land are required in Australia to feed a sheep; or who, knowing this fact, persists in maintaining that these three acres are worth twenty shillings each."[18] But the means of improving their position were at hand, for in 1842 the agitation for self-government culminated in the establishment of the first largely representative legislative council in New South Wales; as a result, improvements in the squatters' position, begun under new Land Purchase Regulations in 1844, were greatly enhanced by Orders in Council in 1847, made under the authority of the Imperial Waste Lands Occupation Act of 1846, which granted security of tenure, "independent" valuation of holdings, and rights of pre-emption. Leases were graded between one and fourteen years according to the degree of settlement of the land, and the pre-emptive right excluded all others during the duration of the lease, though land could be reserved for public use.

Thus, the pastoralists stood triumphant in 1847, but, partly owing to the gold rush of 1851, the demand for complete self-government became irresistible and, under the legislation of 1855, was inaugurated in New South Wales, Victoria, South Australia, and Tasmania in the following year. The landed interests were now on the defensive; led by W. C. Wentworth, who detested what he regarded as these "Yankee notions" of democracy, they tried to build conservative barriers into the new constitution of the mother colony of New South Wales to protect its "great interests,"[19] but by 1858 these were swept away in favor of the secret ballot, a redistribution of electoral districts, and manhood suffrage. A similar course of events took place in the other colonies. Seldom indeed in human history can a would-be governing class have lost political power so soon after attaining it.

But their economic power remained, and to this the avid eyes of the triumphant democrats soon turned in a manner to become increasingly familiar in the next hundred years throughout the world; stimulated by the great new demand for foodstuffs, which were actually being imported at this time from California, and by American land policies, their attention was fixed upon land legislation. In South Australia, where circumstances of soil and climate were favorable and where a squatter class had never overlaid original principles of "systematic settlement," the area under crop, mostly in moderate-sized arable farms, increased between 1850 and 1884 from 65,000 to 2,760,000 acres. But in the other colonies "economic fact warped" this "well-meant effort to follow the precedents of the American prairies."[20] The New South Wales history may be taken as the most typical, for "In all but one of the Colonies the story varied only in detail, with the differences of local geography and politics."[21]

There the effort to "unlock the land"[22] held in the grip of the pastoralists, by "bursting up the big estates,"[23] was inaugurated in two Crown Lands Acts of 1861, which allowed anyone—man, woman, or child—to select freely before survey from 40 to 320 acres at one pound per acre. Thus, a deposit of only ten pounds was the sole essential down payment needed, for payment of a quarter of the purchase price, that is five shillings an acre, obtained a freehold title; and the only conditions were residence for a year, improvements to the land to the value of a pound an acre, and payment of the balance due to the Crown within three years, a provision taken lightly enough by the selectors' representatives in the legislature of the colony. There was a corresponding curtailment of the rights enjoyed under pastoral leases, though a limited privilege of pre-emption was granted to the squatters. Though there were amendments, chiefly liberalizing terms of payment and enlarging maximum permitted holdings, the basic principles of the system remained unchanged for a quarter of a century.

Yet this system of "free selection" failed almost entirely in its attempt to establish a thriving yeomanry. Partly it was prevented by economic circumstance and partly by the resolute and often unscrupulous use of their economic position by the squatters. A royal commission in 1883 discovered that while 29 million acres had been sold since 1861 in New South Wales, the area under crop had increased by less than 500,000 acres. Half of the total granted was constituted by 130,000 selections, the remainder being sold under the auction system, which continued to operate alongside the other; of these probably only 18,000 at most were in 1883 held as homesteads in the way intended. Many selections were abandoned; many were used for grazing; many were absorbed by the great pastoralists and pastoral companies. The extent of the failure of the legislation is shown first by the fact that, whereas one acre in every fourteen of freehold had been cultivated in 1861, one in thirty-nine was the figure in 1880, and one in fifty-four in 1891; and second by the fact that by 1881 a mere ninety-six freeholders had estates averaging 84,000 acres each. The pastoralists, by foul means and fair, were able to retain their ascendancy against the efforts to democratize the holding of land, because nature was on their side as well as economic power; not until the last decade of the century was "closer settlement" really able to begin an agricultural revolution in Australia.

But the squatters paid a high price for their victory,[24] for many of them overreached themselves and fell into the hands of those who had the money, the great pastoral companies; ironically enough, too, it was nature that administered the *coup de grâce* to many of them when she showed, as is her way in Australia, that there were times when she did not even favor the grazing of sheep; overstocked "runs" galloped swiftly to ruin in the withering droughts of the nineties. Yet even today wool constitutes between a half and two thirds of the value of all Australia's exports.

There are many detailed but interesting points of comparison between the development of the land systems of the two frontiers; the similarity of the basic technical problems of survey, and of the use, for instance, of the fundamental unit of the square mile; the anticipation of Wakefield in the Virginia "headright" system;[25] the periodic land booms and slumps, and the fever of speculation which from time to time spread to the distant seats of power;[26] and the "politics" involved in the whole business of granting land. There are also similarities which were of the greatest consequence, such as the constant tendency of settlement to get out of step with systematic surveys. Men preferred to select before survey, although this was technically less satisfactory, and consequently, on the American frontier and from time to time on the Australian, particularly in New South Wales in mid-nineteenth century, settlement far outran survey; hence the term "squatting." This process almost always occurred where there was a sound economic basis for swift expansion. Yet another similarity of importance was the fact that in parts, at least, of both lands the English common law of waters had to be transformed entirely in new circumstances of aridity.

And it is, once more, in the West that the similarities are most striking; there in the second half of the nineteenth century the Americans encountered many of the same difficulties that most of Australia experienced. This is perhaps most entertainingly illustrated by the frauds practiced to obtain enough land for grazing purposes in areas where farming was only possible with difficulty and where the maximum size of holdings permitted to purchasers of government land was small; here the parallel between the pastoralists on the two frontiers after about 1860 was truly remarkable. The means used to evade the Homestead and free selection acts were often indistinguishable. Both employed "dummies"—the very word is the same—to select or homestead adjacent plots which could be "bought for a song" and welded into much larger units. Both were required to reside on their land, but the residences which they built to prove it were often of the most curious character; huts on wheels were common in both cases because they could swiftly put in an appearance in any number of places. In both—the term is Australian—pastoralists "peacocked" large tracts, that is to say, took up or bought all the watered plots, thus rendering great surrounding areas useless except to them. In both, there were upon occasion physical clashes between farmers and pastoralists. "Improvements" which were required upon holdings proved often to be equally fraudulent, as when squatters would dump a useless little water tank in their sparselands, or cattlemen would swear that irrigation work had been carried out because they had "seen water on the ground"—in a bucket. In both, timber could frequently be dishonestly obtained, as when "free selectors" stripped their holding of trees for their mere deposit fee and then abandoned it. In both, great distances, lack of conscientiousness in inspecting officers, and the malleability of political representatives in the new democracies made law enforcement extremely difficult. It would be hard to find closer parallels than these.

The West, however, is not typical of the whole of the United States, and between the land-holding systems of the two continental frontiers there remains, generally speaking, a great contrast. The one is predominantly agricultural, and the other is not. The characteristic American frontier, when all is said and done, is that of the farmer; the characteristic Australian frontier is that of the pastoralist. In 1880 the United States had 150 million and Australia 6 million acres of farming land. America has been the land of opportunity for the pioneer farmer;[27] Jefferson's hope of a great agrarian democracy has not been fulfilled, but it has had a certain basis of reality in American history, for small arable holdings have been, if anything has, typical of the dominant areas of the North and Middle West.[28] The dream of Richard Garland,

> When we've wood and prairie land,
> Won by our toil,
> We'll reign like kings in fairy land,
> Lords of the soil,[29]

has been the dream of both Americans and Australians, but in Australia the cold light of dawn repeatedly brought disillusion. The Australian reality—it has seemed a nightmare to the common run of Australians—has been that of the pastoralists, keepers of the sheep upon which Australia's growth has depended; their romance is of a different order:

> That nothing in the ages old
> . . . .
> Could braver histories unfold
> Than this bush story yet untold.
> The story of their westward march.[30]

This major distinction is nicely exemplified in the use of the term "squatter." Originating in the United States to describe "persons who settled upon . . . unimproved lands . . . with the express intention of acquiring titles by occupancy, or of profiting by defects in the legal titles of the rightful owners,"[31] the term passed into Australian use almost at once with the same overtones, magnified in a manner appropriate to a penal colony —"ex-convicts and shingle-splitters" who "had paddocks hidden in mountain gullies—little more than depots for stolen sheep and *rendezvous* for runaway convicts and men of that type."[32] It soon began to lose its directly denigratory air in both countries as squatting became respectable, but the meanings diverged radically at the bidding of nature; in America it came to mean the pioneer farmer, in Australia, the pioneer pastoralist. And so in the end where the one was a bulwark of democracy, to be approved of—and indeed largely to constitute —the people, the other could be, and usually was considered as, an oligarch and a local tyrant and an obstacle to the fulfillment of the popular will.[33] One could wish for no clearer illustration of the main difference in the development of the land of the two frontiers.

5: *Mining and Money*

IF THE FOOD AND CLOTHING derived from the land are its principal reward to man for his labor, it has to offer him also other products which he can come to value more—minerals. Because minerals such as coal and the base metals are not mined much upon frontiers, they are of no concern here. Even somewhat more highly prized metals such as copper hardly come within our purview; but mining for precious metals, particularly gold and silver, has been from time to time pre-eminently a frontier activity, because they fulfill the classic needs of a frontier product, high value and small bulk. Gold had long been the primary object of miners' hopes, and during most of the lifetime of the two frontiers the search for it was stimulated by the acceptance of the gold standard in the monetary affairs of nearly all the states of the civilized world and by their need for a large expansion of their circulating medium. In this they followed the lead of the economically dominant power, Great Britain, though in the case of a great silver-producing country such as the United States, the single metal standard became the subject of bitter controversy.

Not that much stimulus to the search was needed; despite the fact that North America had hitherto produced little compared with South America, the dream of finding gold in great quantities had never quite died out of the American consciousness.[1] The initial Australian attitude was different; the authorities of a penal colony did not welcome the intrusion of so disturbing an element. In 1823 a convict who produced a nugget was flogged for melting down what was thought to be stolen gold, and a like discovery by a much more respectable member of society, a clergyman, was greeted with the words, "Put it away, Mr. Clarke, or we shall all have our throats cut."[2] Even when large alluvial gold fields were discovered in 1851 by E. H. Hargraves, a squatter who had recently returned from California with the object of investigating the similarity of the country around Bathurst to that in the American fields, officialdom was slow to change its tune. Governor La Trobe of Victoria feared that the colony might "parallel California in crime and disorder," and even the *Sydney Morning Herald* forecast "calamities far more terrible than earthquakes or pestilence"![3] But the popular attitude changed, as might be expected, with great rapidity, and within a short space of time events began to follow a course similar to that in the American gold fields.

There was the same physical rush of people from all over the world. Within a little more than one year after the discovery of gold in California in 1848, there were a hundred thousand people there; Australia's population, which had risen from 221,-000 to 437,000 between 1841 and 1851, leaped to 514,000 by 1852, to 793,000 by 1855, and to 1,050,000 by 1858. These immigrants suffered from very similar hazards—from cramped conditions on ships going out, from lack of water on overland journeys, from disappointment and disease on the diggings, and from fantastic local prices, which were the result not only of a surfeit of people and a shortage of the necessities of life but also of the inflationary effect of the gold found by the few lucky ones. The same techniques were employed in the actual diggings on the two frontiers, increasing in complexity as the richest deposits were skimmed off: first the individual "wash pan"; then the "rocker" or "cradle," used by three or four men; and finally methods which needed a small group, such as the "sluice box" or "long tom." But after a very few years alluvial deposits were exhausted, and shafts had to be dug, and eventually steam mills constructed to crush the quartz; for these processes increasing quantities of capital were needed, and so mining more and more became the exclusive preserve of great companies.[4] For the miner himself there was no choice save to give up mining (or at least individual mining) altogether, or to move on to other fields; most turned to other occupations, but a number had gold in their blood, and the lifelong prospector became a familiar figure not only in the literature but also in the life of the two mining frontiers.[5]

Nor was he an international figure only in a metaphorical sense. There was, as we have seen, much movement between the gold fields of the two countries in the early days, and this meant a considerable degree of American influence upon Australia. Not that the traffic was all one-way: it has been estimated[6] that possibly one percent of the whole population of New South Wales went off to join the California gold rush, and it has even been said that one of the reasons for the official decision publicly to announce the discovery of gold in Australia in 1851 was that it was hoped it would stop emigration thither. In this, it was more than successful, for not merely wandering Australians, but many Americans and Europeans from California, took ship for New South Wales. Their influence spread far beyond the gold fields, for the United States was already a great country and naturally served as a powerful example; the intensity of her effect upon Australia the latter could not then hope to reciprocate.[7]

On the fields themselves the debt was specific, and it is claimed that it extended to other spheres than that of pure mining technique. Fitzpatrick states that "Regulations . . . were founded apparently on those practised in California, which in turn derived from the regulations customary in the old Spanish-American goldfields."[8] Shann goes further and asserts that the system by which Australian miners had to purchase a government license was "in accordance with Californian precedents,"[9] but there seem grounds for caution here lest the American influence be overstated. It is, in fact, hard to find anything in the American fields at all closely resembling the Australian purchase of this "miner's right," and despite suggestions to that effect no licensing system, except for foreigners, was ever put into operation. The land law of the two countries had to be specially adapted to meet the new situation of gold mining; the American practice, operative since 1822, of leasing, and not selling, mineral lands was closer to normal Australian practice than were other land laws, but in the forties it was virtually abandoned except in the West, where it was desired to do nothing which would reduce the incentive to gold production. Thus, it seems that no plan such as that of Senator John C. Frémont to "establish police regulations throughout the mining region and levy a small tax upon the miners"[10] was put into effect. In fact, the most remarkable point about the mining laws of California and the West was that they were almost entirely a local development undirected by government: "Mining law upon the American frontier was a spontaneous growth, embodying some of the experience of Welsh and Spanish miners, but mostly representing the practical adjustments reached on the ground by men used to self-government. It differed from the land law in that it was not the work of non-resident legislators or social theorists."[11] There was unquestionably some passage of ideas and institutions from the American to the Australian fields, particularly in the general liberty accorded to the miner to dig, but their application was often not the same, because the whole spirit of the diggings was in some respects different; there is, for instance, no real American parallel to the powerful Gold Commissioners who controlled Victoria's gold fields, and who were symptomatic of closer Australian governmental control.[12]

The colonial government, despite the Eureka Stockade incident (a brief insurrection on the Ballarat field in which the rioters killed totaled only 22, but which was the nearest thing Australia has ever had to a revolution),[13] maintained on the whole very close and effective supervision both over the development of gold mining and over the diggings themselves. When gold was discovered in California, it had, by contrast, no government; the federal government was convulsed in 1850 by the effort of giving it one; and the United States Congress took no action to amend the land law to suit mining conditions until 1866, when in effect it simply recognized the system of *laissez faire* and local self-regulation which had long existed in the mining areas.[14] This possibly led to more rapid exploitation of gold resources in the United States, and to the evolution of detailed procedures, as for instance in the staking of claims, which were influential in Australia, but it was also responsible in part for the disorders which were possible on the American miners' frontier. The admirable spirit of self-government which is epitomized in the Vigilante movement stems from a dominant strain in the history of the American frontier, but, to an even lesser degree than in Canada (whose frontier was almost always more orderly than the American) was this spontaneous self-government necessary in Australia. There was a large and effective, though unpopular, police force on the Australian fields, and, partly no doubt because of this, there was, except for "sly-grog shanties" selling illicit liquor, very little lawlessness. In the light of California's reputation[15] it is interesting to find "Rolf Boldrewood" (Thomas A. Browne) writing, "Not that there was any rowdiness or bad behavior allowed. A goldfield is the wrong shop for that."[16]

Yet in a broader sense, though the Australian gold-mining experience was certainly not a mere reproduction of the American, it did have a profoundly democratic effect upon Australian political institutions. It came too late greatly to affect the struggle for self-government,[17] which was really won by 1851, but it did contribute forcibly to the democratization of the colonial governments, which took place with astonishing swiftness after they had established their independence. It was not solely responsible, and democracy with manhood suffrage would have come in any case, so that there is a tendency among recent Australian historians to "write down" its influence, but there can be no doubt of the powerful stimulus provided by the great inflow of self-reliant individuals seeking their fortune on the gold fields, nor of the pervasive effect of the "digger" tradition, albeit partly legendary, in Australian life. In that tradition there is a detectable vein of American influence: after this date, for the first time, Australians occasionally began to cast more than a passing glance toward the example of the United States.

That the digger influence in Australia was so strong was the natural result of the scale of the gold discoveries relative to the size of the Australian community. In the decade 1851-60 Australia produced 39 percent of the world's output of gold, and the United States 41 percent; in the next decade the proportions were 31 percent and 38 percent, respectively; and they remained not dissimilar until the turn of the century. But whereas the population of the United States in 1860 was 31,440,000, that of Australia was 1,140,000; this not only shows that its population nearly trebled during the decade, a rate of increase not exceeded in America except in the 1630-40 decade,[18] but suggests how stupendous was the impact of gold upon the Australian economy in other ways. It not only invigorated the currency after the establishment of the Sydney Mint in 1855 and vastly increased the wealth of the community, but it provided an alternative export staple to wool. The initial result of the gold rushes was dislocation, but in the end all branches of the economy benefited. They stimulated the movement toward closer settlement, they contributed to the ultimate industrialization of Victoria, and they had an immediate impact on agriculture owing to the tremendous demand for food, while even the pastoralists, despite their initial loss of virtually all their hired hands, increased their output and found that their wool crop had doubled in market value between 1851 and 1861. Gold stimulated the American economy, but not in this fabulous manner. Even in the West, in those areas where most of the American precious metals were, the effect was hardly comparable. For all the similarities, the Australian miners' frontier of the fifties was a unique phenomenon.

When we come to consider the finances of the frontier, we can observe that the impact upon them of the discovery of precious metals is direct and revolutionary, for precious metals constitute the perfect, as well as the literal, cash crop. They alone, it might almost be true to say, automatically and fully solved—as long as the supply lasted—the great financial problem of every frontier, shortage of currency in a perennially debtor community. The debts of frontiers are not to the same degree questions of morality as were the debts of individuals, but are to a greater extent matters of geography, because the frontiers of a civilization bear the burden and the heat of its day. Because the taming of the wilderness was expensive in money as well as human life, and because time was needed for the investment of capital and labor to bring in returns, frontier folk were, by nature, debtors. Socially, this inconvenience expressed itself first and foremost in a shortage of currency, in the constant dispatch of the circulating medium to satisfy their creditors (of the East or of Britain, as the case may be).

This problem of the frontier had very similar manifestations in Australia and the United States, being especially dramatic in early days. In many areas barter long remained important. Foreign coins figured prominently; the Spanish dollar was important in both communities, though more so, of course, in America; guilders, currency of another trading nation, made their appearance in both; so also did many other coins, but all were rapidly driven out of circulation to finance foreign purchases. Many expedients of a similar nature were adopted to prevent this, such as overvaluing the coins in terms of sterling in America, or actually cutting them into pieces in Australia; but to little avail. Paper money of all kinds—ranging from notes of the Bank of New South Wales and notes of the American colonial assemblies, to private promissory notes—was in very wide use; bills of exchange were, of course, common to both, and individual receipts from Virginia tobacco warehouses make an interesting contrast with grain receipts issued by the government commissary in New South Wales. In Australia private notes continued to circulate, despite repeated government orders to the contrary, until the end of the 1840's, when gold and wool went far to solve the problem of currency shortage in the Australian outback. Political independence in the United States eased, but did not cure, the difficulty; the discovery of gold only alleviated it, and silver became the great issue over which the currency battle of the debtor frontier against the creditor East was fought in the late nineteenth century. The demand for the retention of the greenbacks (paper money issued during the Civil war) was a precursor of the bimetallist movement.

But the cry of the frontier people, that they should not be crucified upon a cross of gold, was not purely a coinage question, for frontier communities had wider debtor interests; they early realized that not merely enough, but too much money would be good for them, since the greater the degree of inflation the more easily they could pay off their debts. Those of them who had a direct stake in foreign trade were not always so anxious to reduce the value of the dollar in the international exchanges, but on the whole they were few; the cotton South was an exception to the rule, and the dominant West did not become heavily involved in the export of grain until the 1860's, and then the frontier was not the part of the West from which the grain chiefly came, while the great bulk of it always went to the cities of the United States and not across the exchanges. The pioneer farming communities felt free to demand inflationary monetary policies to the end, but by 1896 that end was near, for the frontier was officially reckoned to be closed; Bryan was the last prophet of a vigorous line.[19]

In Australia the pastoralists were too directly dependent on the export of wool to play a similar role, and the British connection was too close (and the supply of Australian gold too large) for inflationary demands to make headway against the gold standard in the nineteenth century, although the perpetual need of farmers and squatters for credit led Australia, like the United States though to a lesser degree, to go much further than the Old World in the lending of money on the security of land and crops. Australia was longer, more fully, and more directly dependent upon Great Britain than the United States, but both were to a remarkable degree reliant for many years upon British capital, which began to be needed in its greatest quantities in Australia at about the time that the American need began to decline.

But for a period the advance of both frontiers was financed from London, and rested directly upon the structure of British trade and industry. This economic intimacy is illustrated by the repercussions of boom and slump in the three economies. The United States land boom which culminated in 1836 and early 1837 had a parallel in that of New South Wales culminating in 1838 and 1839. Financial stringency in London, produced by heavy American borrowings, began to make itself felt by 1837, and collapse followed in the United States. The foundation of the new settlements in South Australia and Victoria in 1836-37 alleviated the effects upon Australia of the British depression of 1837, which followed that in the United States; but, when there was further British recession in 1839, nemesis came to New South Wales in the form of a severe five-year slump. Similarly, there was a close connection between the American postwar depression of 1865, the Overend-Gurney smash of 1866 in Britain, and the Queensland boom of 1863-65, and slump of 1866, while the recessions which began in the United States and Britain in 1890 were followed by the great Australian depression of 1891.

The details of this complex relationship are not relevant here, but it clearly illustrates the close connection of the two frontiers with their great investment centers, and particularly London. It serves forcibly to remind us that they were both skirmish lines of the civilization of the West as it pressed forward into the undeveloped lands of the earth, and that the new industrial economic life of the Western world had a unity which transcended the varieties of frontier experience at opposite ends of the globe. It was the development of those frontiers which helped to make possible the swift industrialization of Great Britain, and then of the United States and Australia in their turn.

6: Frontier Techniques

THAT INDUSTRIALIZATION, too, made easier, if not possible, the swift advance of the frontiers, for it provided many of the techniques for efficient exploitation of the resources of the new lands. This is not to say that the inhabitants of the frontier contributed nothing in the way of means to master the wilderness more easily, but it is true that, as Isaiah Bowman puts it, "Pioneer living means a low degree of control by the land settler over instruments of power." The pioneers turned to the civilization at their backs for the technical improvements which expedited their task, for "The full enjoyment of such instruments means modern power civilization."[1] The development of these techniques of the frontier in the two countries provides a number of fascinating parallels, some of which are the result of direct imitation or transmigration of ideas, and some of a similar but independent reaction to similar circumstances—a reaction made easier, it should not be forgotten, by the common source of British tradition from which both originally grew.

Among the most important of the technical developments of the nineteenth century were those in transport, of which perhaps the most significant was the railroad, particularly in the West of the United States, where great distances had to be crossed without much aid from rivers; there "the economic necessity of connecting two opposite coasts which serve two areas of transoceanic commerce"[2] led to the rapid development of the transcontinental lines.[3] The connection of this with the seemingly irresistible Westward Movement of the American people is apparent; and both are lacking in Australian history, where it is symbolic that bushmen pushed "out," as opposed to the pushing "on" of the American backwoodsman.[4] Another reason for the slowness of Australian railroad development was that the poverty of much of the soil made the land grant system impracticable there, as it might very probably have been in the United States west of the 98th meridian had it not been for the importance of "through freight" to the Pacific coast (and even so the first transcontinental line had to be heavily, if indirectly, subsidized by a government guarantee of large loans). Yet railroads were essential to the full development of Australia, and so the government had to step in, for it alone could raise the money for such enterprises in the British market or stand the possible losses, which, as British investors well knew from experience, were by no means unknown to American railroads. The demand which arose in the American West in the last quarter of the century for the control by the state of the great railroad monopolies, which held the populace economically in the palms of their hands, had no counterpart in Australia, where the government had controlled them from the beginning; there the problem was in fact the opposite one of deciding how great a subsidy, direct or indirect, the railroads ought to be given by the state.

Before the railway locomotive there had come the seagoing steamship and the river steamboat. The importance of the former in Australian development has already been noted, and we have touched upon the supreme significance of the river boats in America in the first half of the nineteenth century. There could be no parallel in Australia to the river steamers of the Mississippi Valley, save for a very wan reflection on the Murray, and less than a thousand miles of even that solitary Australian waterway are navigable, whereas the valley of the Mississippi contains 15,000 miles of streams navigable by large river craft. The construction of canals was not really possible in Australia because of the sheer lack of water.

In only one form of modern mechanized transport is Australia highly developed relative to her population and area—aviation. Perhaps because she has come late upon the scene, as well as because geographically and climatically she has great advantages for flying, she has moved very fast in the air and has done much pioneer work in isolated frontier areas. Not only has she established a system of medical care by light aircraft, publicized as the "Flying Doctor" service,[5] but she has also begun to experiment on a considerable scale with the flying of cattle to distant markets direct from outlying districts such as the Kimberleys of Western Australia. In the air, Australia's frontier has found a real means of softening the harshness of pioneer life.

To match the parity of achievement between the two countries in this most modern means of transportation, it is necessary to go back to much more rudimentary techniques, in the days before the effective arrival of the steam engine; the horse and the ox are almost equally important in the history of both frontiers, the mule being less in evidence in Australia. On both frontiers, and particularly in the West as far as the United States is concerned, was bred a race of horsemen; this hardly needs emphasis in the land of the cowboy, but the stockman is not so well-known a figure, and it must be remembered that, as Miles Franklin put it, "The whole population [of the outback] took to horse . . ."[6] But both found that the ox, traditional draft animal of Europe, was better for heavy work than the horse; in the words of a character of Katharine Susannah Prichard: "Horses is all right in their place . . . But the Karri's not the place for them. You've got to get the work out of bullocks . . . Horses has got the spirit on short distances, but they can't pull like bullocks. Horses is all right for a spurt, but they knock-up in no time. And they cost more in feed than they're worth."[7] So in the outback and on the prairies the bullock dray and the Conestoga ox wagon, themselves very much alike, became the principal means of moving all heavy or bulky goods; so, too, the "bullocky" with his stock whip drove the one and the "bullwhacker" with his bull whip drove the other, and both progressed for a steady ten or twelve miles a day, following a daily routine remarkably similar and becoming legendary, even in their tough environment, for a vivid profanity. Australia had nothing to equal the great American firm of Russell, Majors and Waddell, which in 1858 operated 3,500 covered vehicles and owned 40,000 oxen, but its bullock wagon remained for a much longer period a characteristic Bush spectacle.

It is not easy to decide whether this parallel was one of imitation or not, but in the sphere of swift transport of men and light goods, American methods had a direct and distinguishable influence in Australia. The "bush coach" and, as its name implies, the "American buggy" of Australia were American importations. Their large, broad wheels, their wide iron tires, and their light bodies swung on strong leather braces enabled both to drive relatively fast on—or off—the so-called roads of Australia and the American West. They were introduced into Australia in the late 1850's, quite soon after their appearance in America; in the case of the Bush coach this was done by the firm of Cobb and Company, originally founded by four Americans, and brought to prosperity by a fifth, James Rutherford. By the mid-1860's Cobb and Company flourished as much as its American counterpart, the Butterfield Overland Express, and whereas the latter was relegated to a secondary place by the transcontinental railroad in 1870, the last coach in the Queensland Bush did not cease running till 1924. In the case of another transport innovation on the two frontiers, however, there seems to have been no connection whatever, but merely a similar response to similar stimuli—the bizarre experiment of introducing the camel into the deserts of Australia and the United States. Jefferson Davis as Secretary of War was responsible in America, but the beasts never caught on and were obviously destined to rapid extinction at the hands of the railroad in any case. In Australia, which has more desert, they lasted longer and were more used, but in the end succumbed to the same competition, and—by this time—to the added threat of the automobile.[8] But the coming of the camel certainly points the moral of the aridity of Australia and the American West.

In communications, as well as transportation, the techniques developed by the industrial society of the Atlantic Basin aided, though to a less degree, the movement of the frontiers. There was no Australian equivalent to the pony express, which, as Billington says, was "richer in romance than profits,"[9] even though it had a lively through-traffic in mails to California. The overland electric telegraph line constructed by the South Australian government between Darwin and Adelaide was more than its equal in profitlessness, for its shilling a word certainly rivaled the pony express's two to ten dollars an ounce; and not many words were needed with a place as remote as Darwin. In the United States, however, the transcontinental telegraph not only displaced the pony express in 1861, but was a paying proposition, which reduced delays in the transmission of information to the frontiers through which it passed from days to a fraction of a second. Australia's pioneer work in communications was in radio; her production of a cheap, small, long-distance, two-way wireless set in the interwar years, like her development of air transport, cushioned the rigors of frontier existence.[10]

In much more primitive days than these, however, the techniques of frontier living afford close analogies between the two countries. The pioneer's first home in either might be a tarpaulin on poles or a brushwood lean-to, followed by a log cabin or, in the milder Australian climate, a split slab hut, each with a stone or mud chimney and a roof of thatch or bark; in many places they would have shutters and loopholes by the chimney, in case of native attack. The preparations for the first crop equally entailed clearing the ground if it was timbered, usually by the process called "girdling" in the United States and "ring-barking" in Australia; or alternatively trees might be felled and "fired," and the ground "burnt off"; then would come the sowing of the first crop and (later in Australia) of a "truck-patch" of vegetables. Both pioneers would "butcher" the land unmercifully, being naturally concerned only with what they could wrest from it through their simple harvest.

In the cattle country, too, frontier methods were much the same. Branding, ear clipping, mustering, and the technique of handling stock with horse and rope were common to both. The Colt revolver was somewhat less called for in the Australian Bush, but the rifle had its place. The talk of cattlemen today is still the same in the Northern Territory as in Texas—talk of water, feed, stock routes, and even of those who are not above acquiring cattle by foul means as well as fair.[11] In both cases, the American invention of barbed wire has been an essential element in ranch or station development, though ordinary fencing, often of plain wire, was becoming an essential of sheepherding in Australia as early as the 1850's, twenty years before the coming of the barbed variety on the Great Plains.

In agriculture also these middle years of the nineteenth century saw an increasing number of technical advances on both frontiers which owed their impetus to the great technological progress which the Western world was making. There were many improvements to the plow in both countries; the "stump-jump" plow, invented in Australia in the sixties for cultivating very rough ground, was matched in 1868 by James Oliver's chilled iron plow, with its smooth surfaced moldboard for turning the heavy sod of the prairie, and by the American spring-toothed harrow which was produced in the next year; at about the same time the Australian seed drill and a number of American grain drills came into use. There were manifold developments of this kind in the United States, such as the McCormick reaper, but it was not till the 1880's in California (and a decade later elsewhere) that a "combine" both harvested and threshed the grain, whereas Ridley's stripper, which stripped the wheat ears from the standing wheat in a manner eminently advantageous in a hot, dry climate, was invented in 1843 and came into common use in South Australia during the acute labor shortage produced by the gold rush of 1851, in the same way that the Civil War had vastly increased the use of the mechanical reaper in the United States.[12] The Australian William Farrer's development of drought- and disease-resistant wheats in the nineties had plenty of American analogues in the era of the birth of dry-farming techniques, and Farrer corresponded with M. A. Carleton, who had charge of rust-in-wheat research at the United States Department of Agriculture, which was formed in 1862. The American government was prepared to spend money on the encouragement of agriculture somewhat earlier than the Australian, as the provisions of the Morrill Land Grant Act for agricultural education in 1862 show.[13]

This gave an added impetus to American ingenuity and inventiveness in mastering the natural problems of the agricultural frontier, which was already one of their principal characteristics in this as in other spheres of activity. Such developments were indeed cumulative in the United States as she seized the supremacy in that Industrial Revolution upon which they essentially depended; the high degree of control over the instruments of power, which facilitate the transformation of the frontier, came more and more naturally to industrial America, with her growing capital resources as well as technological skills. Australia could not compete in this sphere, and that is the fundamental reason why her development has been slower even than that of the most arid areas of the American West, which was able to profit by the vast overspill of American money, resources, and techniques from richer areas. Thus, it is that the United States is in the process of conquering her deserts in a manner unprecedented in the world.[14]

But she also has, even in this matter, natural advantages which Australia does not enjoy; this is nowhere more clearly to be seen than in the progress of irrigation—first step in the conquest of the desert—on the two frontiers, for the altitude of the West provides water on a scale which is huge compared with that which can be derived from the mountains of Australia. Water somewhere is equally necessary for large-scale and local irrigation, but for the latter Australia's ground—and more particularly artesian—waters do provide her well, better probably than the Great Plains. For its full utilization, however, the invention of the water-pumping windmill was necessary; perfected in America by 1873, it seems likely that it was introduced into Australia very shortly afterward. On ranches and stations, stock routes and stock yards, selections and homesteads, it became almost the commonest sign of the hand of man in both Australia and the American West, equally important for feeding stock and cultivating a vegetable garden.

Windmills and wells, when mass-produced, could be brought within the financial means of the individual, but large-scale irrigation is virtually impossible without state assistance; even co-operative effort has not really been successful except in the case of very small enterprises. This need for the intervention of government is not only due to the great cost of irrigation works, but also to the fact that the power to control the actions of whole communities is essential to the work of artificial irrigation. The American bias against state enterprise in the nineteenth century was one of the reasons for the slowness of the American West in beginning irrigation on a substantial scale, though the continued existence of less arid lands available for occupation was certainly another. It is fascinating to realize that the only considerable and fully worth-while irrigation in the nineteenth century was that accomplished by the Mormons at the foot of the Wasatch Range, which began as early as 1850. That this was so was due to the fact that they were the first real inhabitants of the arid West and were debarred from better lands by the unpopularity of their faith, and also to the fact that the Mormon church, initially under the direction of that forceful genius Brigham Young, was able to play the part of the state, by taking possession and controlling the distribution of all the available running waters. Mormon irrigation was a triumphant success.

But the Mormons were exceptional also in that they alone practiced irrigation actually on the frontier. It is true that later irrigation works expanded the frontiers of settlement, but they did so in reality after the frontier proper had passed; the very need for state aid tends to mean that irrigation is not properly a frontier phenomenon. It is characteristic, for instance, of the situation in both countries that Australian irrigation really started with a Royal Commission set up by the government of Victoria—a commission whose principal member, Alfred Deakin, later Prime Minister of the Australian Commonwealth, visited the United States in 1881 to study irrigation there. His report was very influential, but it was some time before any great projects were under way; they had to await, in fact, the coming of the Federal government. In the end, however, it became the order of the day in both lands, though its possibilities were much greater in the United States.

But even here in the sphere of irrigation, where the technical skill of the Western world exerts itself to the utmost to overcome one of nature's greatest difficulties—aridity—and where it has been rewarded with a success (whatever its cost in financial terms), which no one who has seen the green man-made oases amidst the sands of the desert, or the rice fields flourishing in the dry and thirsty lands of California and the Riverina, can for a moment doubt—even here the comparison of Australia with the United States serves as a sober reminder of how much man is still at the mercy of his environment. There are limits to the present possibilities of irrigation in the United States, but in Australia they are far more circumscribed. In the end one must revert to the fact which is fundamental—that Australia is the worst-watered of all the continents.

7: *Effects of the Frontier*

LET US NOW try succinctly to reproduce the main contentions of the Turner thesis on the effects of the frontier and to assess them in the light of the Australian experience. When we have done so, we may be able to see a little more clearly how much that thesis is weakened or strengthened thereby.

First let us consider Turner's opinion that, "The frontier is the line of most rapid and effective Americanization." "In the settlement of America," he writes, "we have to observe how European life entered the continent, and how America modified and developed that life and reacted on Europe." At first, "The wilderness masters the colonist": then, "Little by little he transforms the wilderness, but the outcome . . . is a new product that is American . . . Thus the advance of the frontier has meant a steady . . . growth of independence on American lines."[1]

Plainly, speaking in general terms, the parallel with Australia is very close. The Australian continent has produced, in like manner to the American, a society quite different from that of Britain, which has in due time reacted on the mother country. Thus, to cite but two instances, Australia has developed a language which is very nearly as different from the mother tongue as is that of America,[2] and she has attained a political independence which is complete except for such connections, within the framework of the British Commonwealth of Nations, as it is her positive will to retain. It is true that some of these connections are powerful links, such as Australian loyalty to the Crown[3] and the staunch, deep, even conservative, Briticism of most Australians, but they wear their ideas with a difference; they pride themselves on being "Independent Australian Britons," a classic phrase strangely reminiscent of that in which the independent Texans described themselves as

82

"North American frontier republicans." The speed at which Australia gained her independence was even greater than that at which the United States gained hers—Australia obtained it in effect sixty, instead of one hundred and sixty, years after foundation—but this emphasizes rather than detracts from the force of the Australian-American parallel.

Yet there are differences, which are worthy of note. At first, for instance, the Australians, so many of whom were convicts, were remarkably slow to try and master their wilderness; it took them a quarter of a century to break out of the narrow confines of Sydney, a fact which can hardly have been due solely to the difficulty of the terrain, but which must have owed much to a lack of desire to do so.[4] When the expansion of the frontiers of settlement did begin, Australian society as a whole, including its frontier areas, remained far more dependent than had the early American colonies on the long arm of the state and on contact through the growing cities of the coast with British supplies and markets. Only their good fortune in being born in the age of the Industrial Revolution enabled them to exploit the continent so swiftly.

In part, this accounts for another important difference—that the frontier was the most effective agent of Australianization for a more limited period than in the United States. It was so at first—perhaps until after the pastoral ascendancy was brought near its end by the gold rushes—but urbanization was already far advanced by this date, and thenceforth became increasingly important. As a higher and higher proportion of Australians, immigrants as well as those born in the antipodes, came to reside in the great coastal cities, these became the chief areas of Australianization. This can be illustrated in the political movements for independence and democracy; the former, which was successful by the middle fifties, was on the whole dominated by the pastoralists, but the latter, which so swiftly took control thereafter, was broadly speaking the product of an alliance between the immigrants—not by any means all of whom were still diggers on the mining frontier—and the city members. The balance of power had already begun to shift into urban hands, and there it was to remain. Rural areas are not frontier areas, but they are likely to be the areas where frontier influence remains most potent. Yet, despite this urbanization, the Bush influence persisted long in Australia: as Crawford writes, "The Australian legend has been predominantly a bush legend . . ."[5] Characteristic are the words of the most Australian of all literary works, *Such Is Life,* by Tom Collins: "It is not in our cities or townships, it is not in our agricultural or mining areas, that the Australian attains full consciousness of his own nationality; it is in places like this, and as clearly here [the Riverina district of western New South Wales] as at the centre of the continent. To me the monotonous variety of this interminable scrub has a charm of its own . . ."[6] Here obviously is a counterpart of the frontier concept in the United States, yet the reality of frontier predominance in the making of Australia seems to have lasted only about a third of Australia's life, whereas in Turner's view the American frontier was the making of the United States for at least three quarters of hers. It is true that what people believe themselves to be is often as important in determining their actions as what they actually are, but it is still of great importance that Australia has always been more highly urbanized than the United States; it warns us that we must be prepared for the fact that the cities were to be the chief Americanizing areas in the last twenty years (and probably even more) of the "new immigration" into the United States. But the undoubted Australianizing tendency of the outback does seem to suggest that the American frontier may have been, if not as Turner claimed *the,* at least *a,* line of most effective Americanization.

Turner also considered that the democracy of the frontier "has been from the time of its birth idealistic . . . The existence of this land of opportunity [the West] has made America the

84

goal of idealists from the days of the Pilgrim Fathers."[7] In their
"optimistic" confidence they "looked to the future." "They had
faith in themselves and their destiny."[8]

Critics have noted that Turner not merely observed this
optimism, but shared it, and he is indeed a warm, often lyrical,
sometimes splendid, exponent of this spirit, which does not
seem to be a cause for lamentation, since it makes him a highly
perceptive historian of the Westward Movement. This idealism,
this looking to the future, is unquestionably a fact. As an Englishman wrote in 1821: "Other nations boast of what they are
or have been, but the true citizen of the United States exalts his
head to the skies in the contemplation of what the grandeur of
his country is going to be."[9] And then he continued in words
quoted by Turner himself: "Others appeal to history; an American appeals to prophecy and with Malthus in one hand and a
map of the back country in the other he boldly defies us to a
comparison with America as she is to be . . ." It is at least
arguable that, a hundred and thirty years later in the midst of
the disillusionments of the "terrible twentieth century," this is
still the keynote of the American character. America has justly
been called "the great experiment," but what Hancock wrote of
all emigrants is pre-eminently true of hers, that they came "not
. . . in despair, but in hope."[10] The invocation engraved at the
foot of the Statue of Liberty was more than a form of words.[11]

This could be the Australian mood also: as a character in
Xavier Herbert's novel of the Northern Territory, *Capricornia,*
says: "We're a great people, we Australians. There's nuthen to
touch us in the World. Course every race says that about
'emselves. But there is something special about us. And what's
given it to us is our freedom from slavery to industry and our
sunshine and our elbow-room. For them three things no race of
people on earth comes near us."[12] This spirit was very strong
at the turn of the century, in the heyday of the *Sydney Bulletin,*
with its motto of "Australia for the Australians," when Bernard
O'Dowd wrote of his hope:

That culture, joy and goodliness
Be th' equal right of all.
That Greed no more shall those oppress
Who by the wayside fall.[13]

But this strain was not always dominant in the Australian character, and at another time O'Dowd himself could ask:

A new demesne for Mammon to infest?
Or lurks millenial Eden 'neath your face?[14]

Ever since the "amazingly simple optimism" of the first settlers has gave way to "frustration" and that "irritability, so often remarked, of colonial society,"[15] this air of reservation has seldom been wholly absent from Australians' opinions of their own country, although few were as outspoken as visiting Englishmen. Not for long did Australians echo the blunt judgment of Marcus Clarke: "The Australian mountain forests are funereal, secret, stern. Their solitude is desolation. They seem to stifle, in their black gorges, a story of sullen despair. No tender sentiment is nourished in their shade . . . All is fear-inspiring and gloomy. No bright fancies are linked with the memories of the mountains. Hopeless explorers have named them out of their sufferings—Mount Misery, Mount Dreadful, Mount Despair."[16] Even Clarke relented, and Australians as a whole came to love their native landscape, but this sense of frustration has never quite departed.[17] Australian humor, for instance, has justly been dubbed sardonic, and in it hope is never allowed to get the upper hand too completely; as Lawson wrote, "There is something sad and pathetic about . . . all bush jokes."[18] Nature enforces this tone: "Out here [in the bush], it can look more like rain without raining, and continue to do so for a longer time, than in most other places."[19] Nature also enforces the tone of complaint, the "bush growl, born of heat, flies and dust,"[20] for to only two small groups of Bush Australians has she allowed swift and great good fortune—lucky gold miners and successful pastoralists.

There is a strong counterstrain of idealism to this touch of cynicism, it is true, centering around the great theme of the advancement of the working man and his solidarity with his mates, which is symbolized in the Australian doctrine of "mateship," but this never entirely overlays the other sentiments. The idealism is embodied in the figure, for instance, of the socialist William Lane, and it is not without significance that he eventually abandoned Australia on a wild and sanguine venture to set up a co-operative, communist settlement in Paraguay. The peculiar dualism is best illustrated by a passage of Lawson's: "And I've carried swag[21] for months out back in Australia—and it was life, in spite of its 'squalidness' and meanness and wretchedness and hardship, and in spite of the fact that the world would have regarded us as 'tramps' . . . The Australian swag was born of Australia and no other land—of the Great Lone Land of magnificent distances and bright heat; the land of self-reliance, and never-give-in, and help-your-mate . . . The land I love above all others—not because it was kind to me, but because I was born on Australian soil . . . Australia! My country! Her very name is music to me. God bless Australia!"[22]

Not too much must be made of this contrast with the United States, for it is most interesting to observe that much of the West once more provides an exception to the American norm; its spirit is surprisingly akin to the Australian. Hamlin Garland and O. E. Rölvaag, for example, write in a vein not unfamiliar in Australian literature, for they set out to depict the life and spirit of man in a dry and thirsty land. When Garland wrote of "The Farmer's Wife," who was "Born an' scrubbed, suffered and died,"[23] his words are reminiscent of many characters in Australian fiction, such as the woman in Henry Lawson who "had been in the bush for fifty years, and had fought fires, droughts, hunger and thirst, floods, cattle and crop diseases, and all the things that God curses Australian settlers with."[24] The finding of Per Hansa's body in Rölvaag's *Giants in the Earth,* likewise, has an emotional impact not dissimilar from that of the discovery of the lost child's body in the Bush in the terrible story told by Tom Collins in *Such Is Life*. The dichotomy in Australian sentiment finds an echo in Garland's symbolic words: "The Main-Travelled Road in the West (as everywhere) is hot and dusty in summer, and desolate and drear with mud in fall and spring, and in winter the winds sweep the snow across it; but it does sometimes cross a rich meadow where the songs of the larks and bobolinks and blackbirds are tangled. Follow it far enough, it may lead past a bend in the river where the water laughs eternally over its shallows."[25]

But between the Australian and American frontiers as a whole, the contrast does remain. The optimism of America's frontier certainly aided its swift development,[26] and it was in part at least the product of a frontier which, for all its hardships, could offer great rewards to the pioneer. Nowhere is it better illustrated than in Turner's account of the passenger in his train crossing the Cascades who "was moved to explain his feeling on the excellence of Puget Sound in contrast with the remaining visible Universe. He did it well in spite of irreverent interruptions from those fellow travelers who were unconverted children of the East, and at last he broke forth in passionate challenge, 'Why should I not love Seattle! It took me from the slums of the Atlantic Coast, a poor Swedish boy with hardly fifteen dollars in my pocket. It gave me a home by the beautiful sea; it spread before my eyes a vision of snow-capped peaks and smiling fields; it brought abundance and a new life to me and my children and I love it, I love it! If I were a multi-millionaire I would charter freight cars and carry away from the crowded tenements and noisome alleys of the eastern cities and the Old World the toiling masses, and let them loose in our vast forests and ore-laden mountains to learn what life really is!' And my heart," writes Turner, "was stirred by his words and by the whirling spaces of woods and peaks through which we passed."[27] How different, although it is the same sentiment at bottom, is an equally typical Australian situation, as related by an Australian historian with the same penetration, patriotism, and poetry as Turner! "A characteristic story of Henry Lawson's sketches the mixed crowd of travellers in a New Zealand coach, and among them a disgruntled Australian, who loudly decries his country: 'Why, it's only a mongrel desert . . . I was born there. That's the main thing I've got against the darned country . . .'[28] Why should he go back? But the road is skirting a plantation of gums, and the Australian sniffs—the unforgettable tang of gum leaves burning stings his nostrils as the coach runs past a tramp crouched over a fire of twigs. He turns fiercely upon an Englishman who has mildly echoed his denigrations. He is going home."[29] Yet the difference seems rather to strengthen than to weaken Turner's claims for the idealistic and optimistic effect of the American frontier, because the Australian frontier also bred idealism, although it was of a different type because the frontier also was different.

"But," Turner maintains, "the most important effect of the frontier has been the promotion of democracy here and in Europe."[30] This was due to the removal of the restraining influences of Old World society; the frontier "strips off the garments of civilization,"[31] for "Removal away from the control of the customary usages of the older communities . . . increased the innovating tendency."[32]

Critics[33] have pointed out that the West did not invent much in the way of democratic institutions, but it was certainly a most potent instrument in their spread. It is obvious that there were European, and especially British, advances in democracy which were influential in Australia, but it is also unquestionably true that the Australian frontier, particularly that of the miners, encouraged democratic development in the way suggested by Turner, for the digger legend entered into the very marrow of Australia's bones. The pastoral influence, in some respects, like that of the planters of the South, was oligarchical, but as soon as the control of the mother country was removed democratic tendencies asserted themselves in unmistakable fashion.[34] This sudden democratization in Australia is even more striking than its counterpart in the United States; it is true that the former has retained more of the British heritage than the latter, but many parts of it changed their character with the passage of time, so that, for instance, Lawson could write in reference to the Australian habit of eating a huge traditional English Christmas dinner in midsummer, "We had . . . a sensible Christmas dinner . . . —everything cold, except the vegetables, with the hose going on the veranda in spite of the by-laws . . ."[35] Hancock could go so far as to declare that "in Australia defiance of 'the truculent, narcotic, and despotic past' has always been one of the most popular themes of forward-looking democracy."[36]

The cities did become, by the date of assertive republicanism in the 1890's, the formative areas which gave its peculiar character to Australian working-class democracy, but the Bush had already played an important part in destroying British habits and setting the tone of Australian life. Tom Collins in his autobiography characteristically exclaims, "For there is no such thing as a democratic gentleman; the adjective and noun are hyphenated by a drawn sword."[37] This emancipating function of the Australian frontier he describes at greater length elsewhere: "For this recordless land . . . is exempt from many a bane of territorial rather than racial impress. She is committed to no usages of petrified injustice; she is clogged by no fealty to shadowy idols, enshrined by Ignorance, and upheld by misplaced homage alone; she is cursed by no memories of fanaticism and persecution; she is innocent of hereditary national jealousy, and free from the envy of sister states."[38] The words are the words of Furphy, but the voice might be that of Jefferson. If we may judge by the Australian parallel, we can certainly accept Turner's view that the frontier encouraged the spread of democracy in the United States.

According to Turner this optimistic American frontier democracy has other linked features—the individualism produced by liberty and equality and the self-reliance of the rugged pioneer, both of which spring fundamentally from the widespread economic opportunities provided by the free land of the public domain. The frontiersman of the "raucous"[39] voice, "rejoicing in rude strength and wilful achievement,"[40] owed his success to these "free lands," which "promoted individualism, economic equality, freedom to rise, democracy."[41]

Australians, it may be said, have certainly all the toughness and ruggedness—and raucousness—of the pioneer; their soldiers still show these qualities in very high degree, and they were exemplified on the political stage in the person of the Australian Prime Minister who was closest to the heart of the Australian soldier, W. M. Hughes, the "little digger."[42] Hancock could write in 1930, "The Australians, like the Americans of a century ago, are still preoccupied with useful things,"[43] and accordingly may be accused of having that lack of refinement which British observers so constantly detected in American nineteenth century life.[44] "Art, literature, refinement, scientific administration, all had to give way," Turner wrote, to the "Titanic labor"[45] of opening up the Great West, and the analogy holds precisely in Australia, which fought the same battle against the overwhelming cultural legacy of Britain. Her writers, for example, swung between the extremes of belligerent patriotism and convinced expatriatism;[46] on the one hand the belief, oversanguine perhaps, that

Homers are waiting in the gum-trees now,[47]

and on the other the complaint of Victor Daley,

They leave us—artists, singers, all—
When London calls aloud.[48]

Here the similar effects of the two new lands are very clearly to be seen.

91

The case of individualism and self-reliance is more complex. Australians are certainly self-reliant in one sense, as any bushman must be (and all Australians seem to share in this outback characteristic to some extent): they are handymen from necessity. But how deep does it go? Are they as individualistic as Turner said the Americans were? Of course, Turner's picture of American individualism was too extreme; it must be altered to conform to the co-operative reality of frontier life, its tradition of mutual aid—its "bees," its logrolling, and its hospitality[49]—and to the fact that so many of the individualists were just like their counterparts elsewhere on the frontier. But for all this, individualism and self-reliance were marked features of the American tradition at least till the end of the nineteenth century.

Nor was the tradition without those disadvantages which often accompany individualism, for the weak went to the wall and one hears chiefly of the successes. Australia, on the other hand, has in a sense concentrated its energies on protecting the underdog; the doctrine of mateship, which embodies this aim, is of cardinal importance in the Australian ethos, even if it sometimes stirs the soul of the outsider less than no doubt it should. The Australian conviction is once more epitomized in the words of Lawson, "I've met men behind revolvers and big mustarshes in Califo'nia; but I've met a derned sight more men behind nothing but a good-natured grin, here in Australia. These lanky sawney bushmen will do things in an easygoing way some day that'll make the old world sit up and think hard."[50] This spirit showed itself not merely in the custom of the Bush, but in the readiness of the Australian people to combine in the great trade union movement of which their country was a pioneer. It had political as well as social manifestations, for, where co-operation of this kind was not enough, Australians showed a notable willingness to call upon the political power of the state to aid them, so that, with New Zealand, they led the world at the beginning of this century in legislation protecting the workingman—imposing arbitration of industrial disputes, linking the high tariff with the obligation to pay high wages, and instituting other measures which have come to be associated with the development of the welfare state.[51]

It is tempting to argue that it was the harshness of the Australian environment which produced this workingman's solidarity and this readiness to lean upon the arm of the state; that the problem of the Australian pioneer was the aridity of a "dried up, God-forsaken country,"[52] whereas that of the American pioneer was the opposite one of "the rank fertility of the soil";[53] and that the individual could deal with the latter, whereas the former needed the interposition of a greater power, the state. But this hypothesis cannot be allowed to stand alone: Other factors enter in to help explain the part that trade unionism and state intervention in economic affairs have played in Australian life. One is that class feeling was strong in Australia and had not had time to fade away since the effective severing of the British connection; another is that the tradition of reliance on government inherited from the days when Australia was a mere penal colony was strong; yet another is that it was the urban proletariat, the great city-dwelling majority, which made the rise of the Labour Party possible; and still another is that Australian democracy came at just the right time to feel the full impact of the socialist, if not Marxian, ideas which were developing rapidly in the new industrial society of Western Europe.[54] These potent facts must give us pause and remind us that Australian collectivism was to a great extent a city, not a frontier, phenomenon.

And yet the influence of the Bush was also important, for its effect was to hasten these developments which were already beginning in the urban areas, whereas in the United States (where also they were to come in the end) the effect of the frontier in the lands through which it had passed was to maintain individualist opposition to collectivist tendencies and thus to slow down the trend toward the economic use of the political power

of the state. That city and country in the antipodes combined
to press the workingman toward the assertion of his power
through combinations political and economic was the fact
which gave Australasia for a space the leadership of the world
in matters affecting the interests of labor. The Australian frontier with its uninhibited working-class spirit began to prepare
the ground for collectivist ideas even before the pastoralists lost
their political, let alone their economic, ascendancy; mistrust
of the squatter provided fertile soil for the swift development
of a proletarian party, which gained effective power almost
half a century before its British counterpart. In the whole
Prose Works of Henry Lawson only one squatter, and he a
very small one, gains a word of commendation; as he writes,
"We hate the boss because he *is* boss, but we respect him because he is a strong man."[55] Property easily became less sacro-
sanct in this atmosphere, as a drover reflects in *Such Is Life,*
when he needs a night's feed for his oxen: "God constructed
cattle for living on grass, and the grass for them to live on,
and . . . we've a choice between two dirty transactions—one
is, to let the bullocks starve, and the other is to steal grass for
them . . . I'm sick and tired of studying why some people should
be in a position where they have to go out of their way to do
wrong, and other people are cornered to that extent they can't
live without doing wrong . . ."[56] The *mores* of the Bush are aptly
summed up in "Waltzing Matilda,"[57] with its migrant Bush
worker who helps himself to a squatter's sheep and comes to a
"sticky end" at the hands of the police; and the comment of
a Northern Territorian on it (albeit he is indulging in the exceedingly dangerous habit of quoting a professor) exactly expresses the contribution of the frontier to Australia's peculiar
ethos: ". . . we sort of look on the Jolly Swagman as a cobber
[mate] that's been martyred. Accordin' to the perfessor feller,
we look on stray things knockin' round, such as sheep drinkin'
at a billabong, or anybody else's chooks [chickens], and things
like that, as public property, or rather property of the tribe,

same's the Binghis [aborigines] do things that's knockin' round the bush. So the Jolly Swagman's the typical Australian, doin' just what he thinks is right, like a Binghi spearin' a kangaroo or somebody's bullock. And the Squatter and the Troopers are the outsiders, the imported people, the foreigners, what have a strong sense of property and a different way of looking at things."[58]

This Bush mateship was not only consolidated by opposition to the pastoralists, who retained economic power long after their opponents had attained political control, but it also produced something for which there is no real parallel in the United States [59]—the Amalgamated Shearers' Union of Australia.[60] Shearing labor was provided largely by rural migratory workers who moved south with the season's work, at least from August to December and sometimes nearly all the year round, traveling almost from the Gulf of Carpentaria to Bass Strait. These workers soon developed, in characteristic Australian fashion, a strong sense of comradeship, so that in 1876 Anthony Trollope called them "the nomad tribe of pastoral labourers . . . one of the strangest institutions ever known in a land"; as a result, when W. G. Spence moved on from an attempt to organize the Australian miners and established the Amalgamated Shearers' Union in 1886, his venture was so successful that by 1890 it was claimed that 32,500 shearers were unionized. The great Australian strike, which began in the latter year, was in part caused and also embittered by the action of the shearers, for the combination of maritime, mining, and pastoral workers enabled them to attack Australia's vital woolen trade all the way from the outback stations to the ships. That the strike ended in defeat does not affect the importance of this unique agrarian institution, which was made possible by the central position occupied by wool in the Australian economy and the peculiar cohesion which it gave to the migratory rural workers. Their readiness to combine for economic action had a deep effect upon the whole social out-

look of Australia. It was made easier by the racial homogeneity
of the "new chums" (Jews, for instance, were frequently the
object of racial discrimination among Bush workers), and the
esprit de corps of the "old hands," which produced an outback
collectivism of considerable importance. This showed itself
clearly in the many Bush ballads which were produced in the
second half of the nineteenth century,[61] and Ward goes so
far as to suggest of the "sturdily collectivist spirit" of this
"commonwealth of vagabonds," that "Perhaps their ideas lie
at the root of the collectivist tendencies in Australian legislation and life . . ."[62]

And if once again we turn to the American West, we shall
see the exception which illustrates the rule of the American
frontier, for there, in circumstances of great natural difficulty
for the farmer, particularly from aridity, we find a number of
the same manifestations of collectivism as we see in Australia.
True, some of the other factors at work in Australia—alliance
with the power of the rising urban workers and the popularity
of European collectivist ideas springing from industrialism, for
example—have a similar impact in the United States, for the
two developments are contemporary, but the indigenous elements springing from the geography of the West were plainly
of major importance. The need of farmers to co-operate in
face of nature's hazards found expression in the Granger movement; their fight against railroad monopolies led them to make
use of their political power; and collectivist ideas and demands
for the intervention of government in economic affairs, however
much they ran contrary to the generally accepted American
legend, became widespread and culminated in the powerful
Populist movement. In other words, the political power of the
frontier in American life remained much the same, but the
shape of its needs and the form of its demands were radically
altered by its change of habitat.

Of this Turner was well aware. He perceived as early as
1896 that, "In the remoter West, the restless, rushing wave of

settlement has broken with a shock against the arid plains. The free lands are gone, the continent is crossed, and all this push and energy is turning into channels of agitation."[63] In 1903 he again considered the whole problem:

> Moreover, with the advent of democracy in the last fifteen years upon the Great Plains, new physical conditions have presented themselves which have accelerated the social tendency of Western democracy. The pioneer farmer of the days of Lincoln could . . . strike into the wilderness, cut out his clearing, and . . . go on to . . . independence. Even the homesteader on the Western prairies found it possible to work out a similar independent destiny, although the factor of transportation made a serious . . . impediment to the free working-out of his individual career. But when the arid lands . . . of the Far West were reached, no conquest was possible by the old individual pioneer methods. Here . . . co-operative activity was demanded in utilization of the water supply, capital beyond the reach of the small farmer was required. In a word, the physiographic province itself decreed that the destiny of this new frontier should be social rather than individual.[64]

Comparison with Australia renders this doubly clear, and if we make certain necessary reservations and modifications to Turner's view that self-reliance and individualism are products of the American frontier, we may the more safely accept its application to the most important sector of America's pioneer experience.

The fundamental reason for the social nature of the Australian and Western frontiers is lack of equality of economic opportunity for the individual. It seems apparent from the very close and convincing work that has been done on the subject since Turner's day that the frontier after 1860 was not a direct safety valve for the discontent of the industrial workers of the East,[65] and that frontier farming was hardly possible "with little or no capital," as Turner supposed. Yet the fact remains that much of the American frontier and of the country which it opened up was held by the small farmer;[66] for many thousands of families the frontier offered better possibilities for a good agricultural livelihood on their own land than anywhere else in the world, and this fact sank deep into the American consciousness. In Australia things were vastly different: there, it is almost true to say, the only successful frontier group was the small class of squatters,[67] and even they tended, like the Southern planters, to be in constant debt. The mass of Australians in the outback were not owners of real property but a wage-earning class, and the equivalent of the American inflationary, debtor, frontier farmer was a unionist, labor member of a rural proletariat. Despite the great flexibility of Australian life, class became an integral part of it, in a manner more akin to the European than to the American scene, although the upper class had no real foundation for its power except money.[68]

This class feeling, in a democratic society whose only real distinctions were economic, produced interesting results: it is almost as if the harshness of nature and the lack of economic opportunity for the many led to an automatic and persistent grudge among the mass of the people against those few who did well out of life in a financial sense. Envy of the successful and all uncharitableness toward great achievement are by no means strangers to Australian life, which also displays in high degree the obverse of a clamorous emphasis on working-class rights— restrictive practices in both town and country. Equality is the Australian passion[69]—fetish might not be a misnomer: "Hostility to privilege, dislike of social gradations, hatred of economic exploitation and an abiding scepticism about the claims of those exalted over their fellows were powerful . . ."[70] and constitute in a way a counterpart to the American passion for social conformity. Australia desires to keep all her sons at the same economic level, America to make all hers behave alike. This leveling process in Australia, as Hancock wrote, "is obviously different from that equality which observers from De Tocqueville to M. Siegfried have remarked in the democracy of America. The Australians are not content merely to attack

98

privilege nor to remove the handicaps which birth has imposed upon capacity. Rather, they tend to ignore capacities in their preoccupation with needs. Equality of opportunity implies free scope for natural talent, which must create new inequalities; whereas what Australian democracy desires is equality of enjoyment."[71]

This instinct for equality has been a most effective social force, and it has produced a belligerently proletarian society: if the United States is essentially a middle-class nation, as it may be said that her people consider themselves to be, Australia is a working-class community and proud of it. This way of life, that of what might be called the lowest common factor, has distinct handicaps, for it tends to restrict its own possibilities of progress, but this does not greatly diminish its hold upon the Australian people. It cannot be said that it is solely a frontier phenomenon, but it does have deep Bush roots. It shows itself in an excessive idealization and romanticization of the Australian rural workingman. Lawson, for example, wrote that "the Australian shearers are about the most independent and intelligent class of men in the world,"[72] which, by any standard, is a tall order. At his hands even the "cockey farmer," the small settler who is the classic failure of the Australian agricultural system, becomes a hero: "And yet this careless Australian selector, who is too shiftless to put up a decent fence, or build a decent house and who knows little or nothing about farming, would seem by his conversation to have read up all the great social and political questions of the day."[73] Miles Franklin, in her description of Bush life in *All That Swagger,* sees the problem much more squarely, both in its success and its failure: "His practice of equality with all men was part of a continent-wide experiment, which . . . was to flower in measures of political freedom and protection for the ordinary man which raised the personnel of the Australian working class to an unprecedented level and then left it shoaled for lack of continuing inspired leadership."[74]

The democracy of the Australian Bush differed from that of the American Backwoods, and the type of equality upon which each set its heart differed likewise. There is more than one thread in these traditions, but it seems likely that the most important one was economic; by and large, it was, as Turner said, the availability of fertile free land on the American frontier which made the difference. This is not a reassertion of the safety valve theory, but it does raise a question for its critics, who have proved beyond a peradventure that only very small quantities of Eastern industrial labor ever successfully exploited the free lands of the frontier, but who have not proved either that large quantities of cheap land divided into manifold small farms was not typical of much American frontier development, or that many Americans did not believe with Turner that "free land meant free opportunities."[75] That Eastern employers believed this, and accordingly feared it, is a commonplace of the history of American land legislation; but even more ineradicable is its counterpart, the popular belief that going West was the path to fame and fortune. It is also true that many small farmers did well in the West, and that the moderate-sized farm holding was the characteristic unit of American agricultural development, except in the arid West (and in some degree the plantation South). These beliefs and these facts, indeed, give a solid basis of *psychological* truth to the safety valve theory, for myth can sometimes be almost as effective a motive in human affairs as material need. For the frontier to act as a safety valve for industrial discontent, it is not necessary that many should reach it: it is only necessary that many should believe they can reach it. The importance of heaven in moulding earthly lives does not depend upon the numbers who actually get there. One of the factors making American industrial workers relatively so successful in the nineteenth century in attaining a standard of living unknown in Europe was the confidence that they derived from their belief that America was indeed a land of opportunity for the individual;[76] and because there were many individuals who "made good," America's legend of democratic equality has been one of providing equality of individual opportunity and not of preventing inequality of individual performance.

In Australia, on the other hand, the life which was open to the vast majority of men in the Bush, though it had its advocates, was too unpleasant and too degrading to be of general appeal.[77] Hardship where it may end in the dignity of individual ownership of sufficient land for a good life, as in America, is one thing: hardship which leaves a man still a wage earner is quite another. Thus it was that men huddled in the great cities in Australia from the earliest days, as they were to do later in the United States, and that their ideals became, not those of individual equality of opportunity as in the United States until the closing of the frontier, but of collective equality of enjoyment enforced by joint action.

Behind the ideas lay—and were partly responsible for them —the different environments in which they were bred; and once again, when duly modified, the Turner emphasis on the importance of free land receives confirmation rather than discredit from the Australian comparison.

For the purposes of this comparison, a number of other features of American frontier life singled out by Turner are illuminating: the instinctive propensity of the American frontiersmen to manage their own political affairs, their tendency to lawlessness, their strongly felt and patriotic nationalism, their instinctive wastefulness of nature's resources, their technical ingenuity, and their driving energy.

First, let us consider the fact, as Turner puts it, that the American frontiersman "knew how to preserve order, even in the absence of legal authority";[78] that he was adept, in other words, at setting up simple, even crude, agencies of self-government when settlement outran organization by the proper authorities. These "squatters' agreements," as Billington calls them, "to which pioneers resorted as a basis for temporary self-government whenever their westward march carried them beyond the bounds of orderly society,"[79] have sometimes reached the pages of the history books (with, for instance, the Mayflower Compact of 1620, the Watauga Articles of Association of 1773, and the Vigilance Committees of the mining frontiers), and they result from a strong American reflex. In Australia it has hardly existed. The continuous presence of powerful agencies of government until the attainment of independence—at a time when the Australian population was only a quarter of the size that the American had been in 1783 and when technical developments made the means of control from Britain much more effective—bred a tradition of reliance upon the state; and this was never radically weakened by anything approaching a revolution. Furthermore, as soon as a few squatters did outrun administration, the Imperial government began to move toward the granting of colonial self-rule, thus setting, as in Canada, the pattern for the slow development over the next century of the democratic free association of independent states which is the British Commonwealth of Nations. In this policy of evolution the grip of government was only gradually relaxed, so that there is really no close parallel with the American system of colonization by territorial organizations subsequently admitted as states into the Union. Partly because the rural population of Australia is very dispersed compared with that of the United States,[80] and partly because of its more authoritarian social and political tradition, Australia has never displayed a lively tendency to political organization from below at the basic level of local administration; indeed, it is characteristic that local government in rural Australia is to this day weak, relatively ineffective, and unable to arouse popular enthusiasm and participation.

The American virtue of self-government does, however, when carried too far, tend to become the vice of disregard for the law; the frontiersman was "impatient of restraints," and,

as a result, there developed those "lawless characteristics of
the frontier" which were, as Turner wrote, "sufficiently well
known" in 1893,[81] and which are much more familiar to those
who have grown up in the era of the "Western" in film and
story. This tradition of frontier violence has never had the same
place in Australia.[82] Crime rates have always been high in the
cities. Henry Parkes, who landed in Sydney in 1839, wrote, "I
have been disappointed in all my expectations of Australia
except as to its wickedness; for it is far more wicked than I
had conceived it possible for any place to be . . .",[83] but there
was no large-scale lawlessness of the American frontier type.
It was, for instance, a source of pride to the government that
the gold fields remained so orderly, for New South Wales had
been able to "establish at the beginning the precedent of official law and order."[84] Indeed, it seems not unlikely that the
lack of popular pioneer disorder has been due more to the firm
control of government than to a difference in the instinctive
sentiments of the people: in a one-time penal settlement one
would expect the arm of government to be strong but would
not expect universal support for the agencies of law and order.

The convict origins seem to have issued in a certain Australian mistrust of and contempt for the law; it is as if the effective
control of the state prevented overt manifestations of lawlessness on the part of the populace, and as if, as a consequence,
they assumed an underground and more insidious form. This
is illustrated by the part played by the bushranger in Australian legend, epitomized in the story of Ned Kelly and made the
theme of many a ballad, such as the "Wild Colonial Boy," and
of a number of novels, such as *Robbery Under Arms*. It is
true that Theodore Roosevelt noted much the same thing in
the case of Jesse James: "There is something very curious in
the reproduction here on this new continent of essentially the
conditions of ballad-growth which obtained in mediæval England; including, by the way, sympathy for the outlaw, Jesse
James taking the place of Robin Hood."[85] But in fact the

American outlaw has not been the hero which the Australian bushranger has been; public sympathy has not been as widely in his favor in the lore of the country, whereas much of the glamour of the cowboy in American myth has attached itself in Australia to the bushranger.

And it is not fanciful to see another reflection of this attitude in the wide dislike, hatred is not too strong a word, among Australians (particularly perhaps in New South Wales) for the police, a sentiment which has a long history but which seems visible to the outsider even today. The police force early (and almost necessarily) recruited exconvicts, and had a tradition of "strong-arm" methods of which some contemporary observers still claim to see signs; this tended to make the "trooper" in the eyes of the people the worst kind of "scab," one of the most pungent derogatory terms in the Australian vocabulary. This certainly cannot be regarded as an exclusively frontier phenomenon, for it was quite as pronounced in the cities, but it did have strong manifestations in the outback; the white man's comment on the native tracker in *Capricornia* is symptomatic of this marked suspicion of the police: "His own people would have nothing to do with him; for he was a policeman-born and, like his master—indeed all his brethren of the man-catching profession—, of strange unloving and unlovable nature—actually that of a rogue set to catch rogues."[86] This gives expression to a very general Australian sentiment.

But it goes deeper than a mere mistrust of the police, an enmity toward agents of the law—it amounts to a feeling against the law itself.[87] Once more, Lawson expresses it exactly: "We make (or are supposed to make, or allow others to make) laws for the protection of society . . . and we pay thousands of men like ourselves to protect those laws and see them carried out; and . . . for the . . . punishing of men—like ourselves—who break them. Yet, in our heart of hearts we are antagonistic to most of the laws, and to the Law as a whole . . . and to the police magistrates and the judges. And we hate law-

yers and loathe spies, pimps, and informers of all descriptions
and the hangman with all our soul. For the Soul of Man says:
Thou shalt not refuse refuge to the outcast . . . And how many
of us, in the case of a crime against property—and though the
property be public and ours—would refuse tucker[88] to the
hunted man, and a night's shelter. . . ?"[89] In this curious con-
fusion of pity for the criminal with contempt for the law, even
in Australia's democratic self-governing society, there seem to
be strains derived from its authoritarianism, from its convict
origins, and from its reaction to an environment which allowed
economic success only to the few. In America there is a deep-
rooted mistrust of the state as such, an echo of Tom Paine's
belief that government is at best a necessary evil, at worst an
intolerable one. In Australia, which has been forced by tradition and geography to rely much upon the state, the mistrust,
which is perhaps more baneful, is of the actual agencies of
government, and this produces a kind of political schizophrenia,
with every man hating that upon which he is dependent.

The attitude of the frontier to the state has another and
quite different manifestation in the United States, what Turner
called "the nationalizing tendency of the West."[90] Nearly all
the states except the original thirteen grew up under the aegis
of the Union, and the frontier thus became the chief area of
good feeling toward federal, as opposed to state, authorities.[91]
This was less noticeable in Australia, partly because federation
came long after individual colonial self-government, and partly
because there were many frontiers moving in from the separate
coastal capitals and not one coherent Westward Movement.
Interstate rivalries persisted long in Australia, and even when
the Commonwealth was formed it was largely the work of
urban rather than rural leaders. Yet the frontiers have often
strengthened national movements, as when Western Australia's gold fields virtually forced it into federation at the elev-
enth hour.[92] The common Bush experience unquestionably had
a cohesive effect upon Australian development, for the homo-

geneity of the rural environment helped to forge the sentiment of Australian nationality, while the further men penetrated outback, the weaker became their sense of contact with, or allegiance to, a particular state.

Even closer is the analogy between the attitude of the bushman and that of the backwoodsman to the bountiful resources of nature—their prodigality and wastefulness. At the time that Turner wrote, Americans were becoming conscious that the frontier was closing fast and that ruthless exploitation could not be continued much longer; he expressed it thus, "The cry of scientific farming and the conservation of natural resources replaces the cry of rapid conquest of the wilderness."[93] Of this prodigious output of raw materials from lands opened up by the two frontiers, Great Britain was, in the nineteenth century, a great beneficiary; Australia benefited much, but, because her resources were not so spectacular, it did not do so in quite the dramatic fashion that the United States did. Nevertheless, she too, despite her small population, has had to begin thinking in terms of conservation, the fewness of her numbers being outweighed by the niggardliness of nature. But of the sentiments of her frontier there is equally little question; in the words of Miles Franklin: "No one thought of conserving anything . . . Here was a wonder continent, a vast garden of Eden free from sin and disease, left intact by the aborigines. The aim was to rifle it, exploit it in greedy haste . . . Nemesis was not in that generation, nor the next."[94]

Two final, and linked, features of Turner's frontier thesis are well worth consideration, the technical ingenuity and driving energy developed by American frontiersmen, what he calls "the ideal of discovery, the courageous determination to break new paths, indifference to the dogma that because an institution or a condition exists, it must remain." "All American experience," he concludes, "has gone to the making of the spirit of innovation."[95] This ingenuity is certainly characteristic of American life, and although Yankees elsewhere have contributed much to it, it seems likely that the frontier has been of great importance in its development.[96] The manifold changes of environment—from coastal plain to mountain, from timbered to long-grass to short-grass country, from desert to mountain to West coast valley, from hot south to cold north—have obviously demanded the rapid invention of new techniques. One of the most striking of these changes is the central theme of Walter Prescott Webb's *The Great Plains,* but the spirit which made it possible is common to almost all America's frontiers;[97] it is the classic spirit of the predominant North, and to it in part must be ascribed the American industrial supremacy of the twentieth century.[98]

This unparalleled American capacity for technical innovation and adaptation has no precise counterpart in Australia, where the spirit of the general handyman is its nearest equivalent; certainly Australia has not yet disclosed anything to resemble the technological genius of America. The Australian is unquestionably ingenious; he can—he must in the Bush—turn his hand to any essential purpose. Characteristic is Shann's comment on Bush accidents to the "American buggy"; the driver "was a poor hand indeed if he could not cut a sapling to replace the broken spoke or fix up the broken traces with the aid of the local fencing wire."[99] Of these things the American pioneer was capable also, but he lived in a general atmosphere which made him capable of much more; the element of perfectionism, which is so marked in the American character, is conspicuously absent in the Australian.[100] The Australian substitute for the American passion for mechanical innovation might be described as the spirit—it is one of their favorite expressions—of "give it a go," of making shift with what you have;[101] it is the policy of reducing your needs in order that they may all be fulfilled, rather than of increasing your output in order to meet bigger demands. This contentment with (or grumbling acceptance of) the second-best owes something to the frontier; it is possible to hazard the idea that in an environment which has so many unpleasant, nay grave, emergencies up its sleeve in the shape of fire, drought, and flood (to name but the principal ones), men become reluctant to expend their last ounce of energy upon refinements, lest disaster befall them and they have no reserves of strength to meet it. At least while her national surplus of power remains as limited as it is, an Australian development of her arid lands comparable with the contemporary American conquest of her deserts does not seem very likely, for it is not prompted by the character of the Australian bushman. Lawson's story, "The Iron-Bark Chip," carries the full flavor of this. It tells of a task of fencing in the outback, which the swagmen working at it decide to complete in a hurry with a spurious iron-bark girder, because they are " 'about full of' the job and place" and want "to get their cheque and be gone to another 'spec' "[102] they have in view. This strikes exactly the right note, but even better is the denouement, which tells of the suspicious inspector who finds the fraud, but who puts the evidence of it, a chip from the iron-bark girder, on top of a post—and there forgets it.

For much of the difference lies in the furious energy of American life, which derives in considerable measure from the habits of the frontier; the Westward Movement has no real counterpart in Australia, and neither has the drive which made it possible. As an American character of Lawson's says reflectively to a group of Australians on the banks of the Murray: "When I come over here I calculated that I was going to make things hum, but now I guess I'll have to change my prospectus. There's a lot of loose energy laying round over our way, but I guess that if I wanted to make things move in your country I'd have to bring over the entire American nation—also his wife and dawg. You've got the makings of a glorious nation over here, but you don't get up early enough!"[103] This difference is no doubt partly climatic, for Australia is a hot land, much of it without the stimulus of winter cold.[104] Also no doubt it owes much to the lack of economic opportunity and the wide extension of a rural, as well as urban, wage-earning class; the characteristic Australian bushman was, after all, for many years a shepherd of other men's sheep, and it does seem that between moderate property owning and energy there is a close connection. Other things may have had their effect, such even (though the notion might be sharply resented) as the British ideal of the leisured gentleman; and the Australian-American contrast must not be exaggerated, for the Australian in case of dire necessity (of which there is plenty in the Bush) is capable of remarkable feats of endurance. But spontaneous, or even socially induced, energy is not the Australian norm: "go-getting" is not a virtue in Australian eyes. Here is a real difference. The opening words of what would have become, had it been completed, the greatest epic poem of the American frontier, Stephen Vincent Benét's *Western Star,* are—"Americans are always moving on."[105] The opening words of the most typical of all Australian books about the Bush, *Such Is Life,* which set the tone of the whole work, are—"Unemployed at last! . . ."[106]

Thus, once more we can say that some of Turner's contentions about the effects of the American frontier, such as its wastefulness of nature's resources, have exact counterparts in Australia; that others have equivalents in which modifications are produced by local conditions, such as the attitude of the frontier to law and order; and that yet others, such as American energy, where there are wide divergences, may perhaps be explained by differing circumstances.

8: *Turner and Two Continents*

WHAT LIGHT, then, does the Australian comparison throw on Turner's frontier thesis? Let it be said first of all that critics have expected too much of Turner; he was one of the great seminal minds of American history, but his ideas, like those of many other great men, needed elaboration and modification. This they have received, mostly at other hands than his, and often, as a result, in a form so radical as to invite us to throw the whole concept of the frontier out the window. Yet absolute consistency is hardly to be expected of any historian. Indeed, as Turner himself clearly saw, man is so much at the mercy of his environment that when the environment is different, so will his ideas be.

Rare indeed are the principles of human behavior which have universal validity in every historical circumstance, and almost any universally applied and internally consistent hypothesis in history arouses the instinctive suspicion of the historian. Thus, it appears that many of Turner's critics have forgotten the existence of the great frontier forest in their minute scrutiny of its trees. In this way, for example, they have blamed him for asserting that the effects of the frontier in American history had made that history unique, although it is obviously true to a considerable extent. Their error is to suppose that this fact is inconsistent with the existence of frontiers elsewhere which produce in some respects a similar set of effects. The American frontier is, indeed, unique in its character and effects; and so is the Australian frontier; and so, no doubt, are the Russian, the Brazilian, and many other frontiers. With these Turner was not concerned; it was sufficient for him to perceive the American application of his frontier hypothesis, though he was doubtless aware of analogous circumstances elsewhere.[1] He specifically wrote, "The United States lies like a huge page in the history of society,"[2] revealing luminously the course of universal history. Even more clearly does he show this appreciation of the existence of differing frontiers by his reiteration of the different forms and effects of the frontier in different times and places in American history, although his critics sometimes ignore this implication of his analysis.

The Australian comparison makes some things plain. The effects of the frontier in Australia are certainly such as to justify amply the essential Turner doctrine, the vital modifying effect of the open frontier, for both peoples were transformed by their raw environment.[3] We may go further and observe that the more alike conditions are, both in respect of the nature of the environment and other factors, such as the character and habits of the people, the more closely do the resulting modifications correspond. In the matter of ruthless exploitation of nature's resources, they are identical; in that of Americanization and Australianization, as well as of promoting democracy, they are remarkably similar. Where there are substantial differences of circumstance, there are substantial differences of effect, although some resemblance remains; thus, the idealism encouraged by the Australian frontier was different from that of America, as were the egalitarianism and the lawlessness, but they have much in common. Where there are wide differences of circumstance, only odd threads of similarity can be seen; thus, of American individualism, American ingenuity and drive, and American instincts of spontaneous self-government, little is to be seen in the reliance of Australians on the strength of the state and their tendency to contentment with that good which is the enemy of the best. Many of these differences can be traced to the geographical fact that the cardinal Turner doctrine of the availability of free land does not apply in Australia. That we can take a hypothesis, such as Turner's, specifically framed for the circumstances of one national history, and find it illuminating, and illuminated by, those of another, is a remarkable tribute to it. With suitable modifications of detail it is greatly strengthened thereby.

The Australian comparison also throws general light on the Turner thesis. It sometimes seems to have been held that because his hypothesis does not apply to all American frontiers at all times, it therefore has no validity or utility; but historical concepts of this kind are not universal laws, they are guides to probabilities. It is clear, for instance, that the frontier of the South produced very different effects from the frontier of the North, and the analogy between the planters and the Australian squatters adds interest to this point. It is clear also that the American West produced very different effects again, and these are illuminated by much of the Australian experience, to which that of the West was so akin. But neither of these frontier areas was dominant in the history of America, and their effects were recessive.

The characteristic American frontier was that of the great Northern and Western belt of the United States, which is very approximately bounded on the south by the 38th parallel. This area, which became finally preponderant in the Civil War and in the years which followed it, long contained and still contains, particularly if California be added to it, the vast majority of the American people;[4] and historically its type of frontier was by far the most important. It was the frontier norm for the United States, this small farmer's frontier, and it was the principal image which Turner carried in his mind. And this concept of the norm of the frontier can be applied in time as well as in place; critics have often tacitly assumed that the frontier at a particular time is the only frontier of importance at that time. Yet nothing could be farther from the truth, or from Turner's idea of it. He likened the United States to a palimpsest, with the frontier's influence embedded at each level: "If, indeed," he wrote, "we ourselves were not pioneers, our fathers were, and the inherited ways of looking at things, the

fundamental assumptions of the American people, have all
been shaped by this experience of democracy on its westward
march. This [frontier] experience has been wrought into the
very warp and woof of American thought."[5] In this sense more
than ever can the frontier of the North be justly considered the
American norm; and of that frontier many, indeed the majority,
of Turner's judgments are in essence true. It was a line of rapid
Americanization, it bred optimism and idealism, it aided the
spread of democracy, it often nurtured pioneer self-reliance and
individualism, it encouraged nationalism, it offered economic
opportunity, it seemed to many in the East a way of escape, it
developed ingenuity and energy—and the heart of it was free
land.

In some of these things the characteristic American frontier
was unique: in others it had parallels elsewhere. A number of
these we have seen in Australia's development; others are
matched perhaps in different areas of the world. One aspect of
it, which Turner noted, is peculiarly fascinating to the contemporary European historian; what he calls its "incessant expansion,"[6] the remorseless, surging movement of the American
frontier to the West. There is no real Australian counterpart
to this compelling dynamism of America which is so fully embodied in the Westward Movement. Tocqueville saw the maj-
esty of this elemental-seeming process: "This gradual and
continuous progress of the European race toward the Rocky
Mountains has the solemnity of a providential event. It is like
a deluge of men, rising unabatedly, and driven daily onward by
the hand of God."[7] In one land alone does the casual eye see
its like, the swift and ruthless Eastward Movement of the great
Russian people to far-off Kamchatka. It would not have been
otherwise than fascinating to an historian and thinker of
Turner's "lively and irrepressible intellectual curiosity"[8] to see,
in our day, these two so-different frontiers meeting upon the
shores of the Bering Sea, in dread competition, each after its

own fashion, for leadership of, or mastery over, the world of
men.

This comparative study of man on two frontiers reinforces
the kind of environmentalism in which Turner believed; men
are to a remarkable degree influenced by their geographical
environment, and particularly those aspects of it which impinge
directly on their economic life.

The conflict between what the geographers call Determinism
and Possibilism would be a barren battle if fought to a finish.
Absolute determinism by physical environment is manifestly
absurd, for what men are and what they bring with them, both
consciously and unconsciously, when they come to the frontier,
have far too great an effect upon their development. Men cannot return to Nature; even Robinson Crusoe had an inherited
character, an inherited physique, and manifold acquired habits,
ideas, and experiences, which made him react in a very different
manner from the Swiss Family Robinson to his new and savage
abode. Only to a very limited extent can the pioneer be born
again. The, in a sense, opposing forces of heredity and free will,
as well as that of previous experience, combine to limit the effect of even so powerful an environment as the frontier.

Nonetheless, its influence is always heavy and can be crush-
ing. Where hereditary characteristics and the experience and
techniques of the civilization from which the frontiersmen have
come are similar, we see in clearer relief the impact of sheer
environment. We should expect greater divergences of development where race and history and experience are widely different; thus, the Australian and American frontiers are likely
to have much more in common with one another than with, for
example, the frontiers of Argentina or of Manchuria, for they are
European in stock, English-speaking in language, and at bottom,
British in tradition.[9]

As we have seen, where in Australia and America geographical conditions are also very similar, the effects of the frontier

114

have been remarkably alike. Thus, the similarity between the American West and the whole of Australia produced analogous results in political and social behavior. The pattern of economic development in areas suitable for the production of great raw-material staples, primarily for the British market, was broadly similar. The attitude of both frontiers toward the native peoples was little short of identical. But where the geographical conditions were different, the effects were widely divergent. The self-reliant, optimistic, ingenious, individualistic, independent American of the pioneer farmer's frontier was markedly different from the socialistic, sceptical, rough-and-ready, "mate-conscious," collectivist Australian of the rural wage-earner's frontier. Here the distinction is so clear-cut as fully to justify the weight which Turner gave to the effect of the frontier environment.

And we are brought back again and again to the central importance of economic life, which Turner embodied in his vital doctrine of free land. The framework of existence on the frontier is that of economic possibility, and finding the economic key in each region is the most important step which its inhabitants have to take. Jamestown and Port Jackson hung on by their fingernails until they discovered tobacco and wool. Subsistence agriculture meant but a miserable existence; missionary zeal could convert native peoples, but not install European ones. Without the means of economic growth even political power was useless, as the failure of free selection in Australia and of plantation slavery in the South, each in their different ways showed. As Turner realized, the proper use and development of land is overwhelmingly important in the life of all frontiers. Its economy is the basis of every frontier's growth, and the limits and direction of that growth are largely controlled by its physical environment.

The limits imposed by environment are always important, but they are also flexible. At the present time they are receding fast, as the instruments of power develop for expediting frontier growth. There is a famous chapter in Webb's *The Great Plains,* called "Some Vagaries of the Search for Water," which ends with a humorous and ironical account of abortive efforts at artificial rainmaking on the Plains.[10] The chapter needs rewriting today: great things may yet be done in Australia with the coming of the rainmakers. In the atomic era there may be virtually no limit to the generation of power, and, therefore, hardly any limit to the extent to which we may transform our environment. It may well be that, as the Russians have claimed, in curiously Biblical language, man may be able by its aid actually to move mountains and water deserts; that the frontiers in the lands of great heat and intense cold may just be opening before us; and that what we have been telling ourselves for fifty years—that the process of occupying the open spaces of the world is ended—may be quite untrue. The frontier may yet be with us for a while. And even if, with deadly irony, that very source of our new power plunges us back once more, through a nuclear cataclysm, into barbarism, there will be—to keep us occupied—frontiers enough and to spare at a far more primitive level than we have seen these many years.

NOTES AND APPENDICES

Notes to Introduction

1. The sociologist tends to the other extreme, as for instance James Graham Leyburn in his interesting comparative study of frontiers, *Frontier Folkways* (New Haven, 1935), p. 4: "Generalization, if it is significant, *must* be by comparison." [Author's italics.]
2. Perhaps we may also avoid some of the pitfalls in the paths of the great comparative historians, who take the history of all mankind as their field of study.
3. As, for instance, George Wilson Pierson in his article, "The Frontier and American Institutions: A Criticism of the Turner Theory," in the *New England Quarterly*, 15 (June, 1942). Much more recently Professor Owen Lattimore has considered "The Frontier in History" in a stimulating general way in *X Congresso Internazionale di Scienza Storiche, Relazioni*, Vol. I, p. 105.
4. One might illustrate, a little whimsically, the degree to which similar phenomena may occur without apparent connection by a glance at one or two frontier place names in Australia and the United States. One might be hard put to it to guess, if one did not know, in which country Kalamazoo or Kalgoorlie was; and it might appear the most difficult of problems to distinguish New South Wales's Wagga Wagga from Washington's Walla Walla, were it not that New South Wales also boasts a Walla Walla.
5. See Gordon Greenwood, *Early American-Australian Relations from the Arrival of the Spaniards in America to the Close of 1830*. (Melbourne, 1944).
6. This sentiment must not be exaggerated, nor unreservedly accepted as applicable at the present time, for the left wing of the Australian Labour Party today shares in full measure the tendency to anti-Americanism characteristic of its counterpart in the United Kingdom, while there have been in the past substantial material causes of friction, such as the American tariff on wool.
7. While I was engaged in splitting logs (still the staple fuel of many Australians, as of many nineteenth century Americans), with my American ax, to heat my house in Canberra (still, like

119

nineteenth century Washington, demanding something of a pioneer spirit from its residents), I was told of a new type of ax, much better adapted for this purpose; it was known as the "block-buster," and was of Canadian origin. It is not likely to be as well adapted as the American ax to the feat, legendary on both frontiers, of shaving its owner upon occasion.

8. *The Sydney Morning Herald,* May 19, 1954.

9. Frederick Alexander, *Moving Frontiers; An American Theme and Its Application to Australian History* (Melbourne, 1947).

10. William Keith Hancock, *Survey of British Commonwealth Affairs,* Vol. II—*Problems of Economic Policy 1918-1939,* Part 1 (London, 1940).

11. Alexander Brady, *Democracy in the Dominions, A Comparative Study in Institutions* (Toronto, 1947); and A. L. Burt, "If Turner Had Looked at Canada, Australia, and New Zealand When He Wrote About the West," *The Frontier in Perspective.* Walker D. Wyman and Clifton B. Kroeber (Eds.) (Madison, 1957).

12. As for example, N. D. Harper, "Turner the Historian: 'Hypothesis' or 'Process'?", *University of Kansas City Review,* Autumn, 1951; and Paul F. Sharp, "Three Frontiers: Some Comparative Studies of Canadian, American, and Australian Settlement," *Pacific Historical Review,* November, 1955.

13. The geographers have long been interested in the subject. See, for instance, Isaiah Bowman, *The Pioneer Fringe* (New York, 1931), and W.L.G. Joerg (Ed.), *Pioneer Settlement* (New York, 1932).

14. See "F. J. Turner and the Frontier in American History," in Harry Cranbrook Allen and Charles Peter Hill (Eds.), *British Essays in American History* (London, 1957).

15. Arnold J. Toynbee, *A Study of History* (Abridged ed.) (London, 1946), p. 43.

16. W.K. Hancock, *Australia* (London, 1930), p. 32.

Notes to Chapter 1

1. There is even more variation in distances given in different authorities for sea routes between the world's leading ports than one would have expected; these figures are derived from *The Times Atlas* (1920), *Philip's Mercantile Marine Atlas* (1935), and *The Canadian Oxford Atlas* (1957).

   Whereas in the few days spent crossing the Atlantic other ships are seen with some frequency, we saw none at all during three weeks on the Pacific. For an Englishman on a first visit, the only experience which I know to match in intensity that of appreciating the vast size of the United States through getting on a fast train and keeping on going West for nearly five days, is that of appreciating the isolation of Australia through getting on a ship in London and steaming for nearly five weeks before reaching Sydney, and then going on for a further three weeks from there before reaching the West coast of the United States.

2. See Harry C. Allen, *Great Britain and the United States, A History of Anglo-American Relations (1783-1952)* (London, 1955), pp. 36-38.

3. This seems to be true despite "the aptitude of colonial youths for the sea" in the early days (R.M. Crawford, *Australia,* London, 1952, p. 57.)

4. It is significant that the great British liners still provide a much-used (and cheap) means of travel between western and eastern Australia.

5. Ellen Churchill Semple, *American History and Its Geographic Conditions* (Boston, 1903), pp. 36-51.

6. Norman A. Graebner has recently emphasized in *Empire on the Pacific* (New York, 1955) the importance of maritime influences in the occupation of California. This must make us correspondingly cautious in emphasizing the terrestrial, or territorial, aspect of Manifest Destiny.

7. The Federal Council of Australasia, set up in 1885, was quite ineffective.

8. Yet the most penetrating of Australian historians applied the term to Australia spontaneously. The opening words of his book on Australia, published in 1930, are: "Many nations adventured for the discovery of Australia, but the British peoples have alone possessed her. For six generations they have swarmed inland from the sea, pressing forward to their economic frontiers, which are the only frontiers Australia knows." Hancock, *Australia,* p. 11. Ten years later he wrote: "I used the idea of the moving frontier in Chapter I of my book, *Australia . . .,* without any conscious borrowing from American historians, with whose work I was not then familiar." Hancock, *Survey of British Commonwealth Affairs,* Vol. II, p. 4 note.

9. Miles Franklin, *My Career Goes Bung: Autobiography of Sybylla Penelope Melvyn* (Melbourne, 1946), p. 49.

10. Brent of Bin Bin, *Up the Country; a Tale of the Early Australian Squattocracy* (Sydney, 1951), p. 1.

11. Hancock, *Australia,* p. 11.

12. Thomas Griffith Taylor, *Australia; A Study of Warm En-*

vironments and Their Effect on British Settlement (London, 1940).

13. Floods, alternating with the droughts, are among the great menaces to Australian life.

14. Including the Darling and the Missouri.

15. Henry Lawson, *Prose Works,* Vol. I (Sydney, 1937), pp. 336-37.

16. Taylor, *op. cit.,* p. 250.

17. O.H.K. Spate, "Australia, The Land and Its Limitations," lecture read in manuscript.

18. Taylor, *op. cit.,* p. 20.

19. *Ibid.,* pp. 4-5.

20. McDouall Stuart's reaction when he crossed Australia from south to north, ". . . greatly delighted to behold the water of the Indian Ocean in Van Diemen's Gulf . . . I dipped my feet and washed my face and hands in the sea . . .," may be compared with that of Lewis and Clark on the shores of the Pacific, "that ocean, the object of all our labours, the reward of all our anxieties." (Quoted in Ernestine Hill, *The Territory,* London, 1952, p. 77, and Ray Allen Billington, *Westward Expansion; A History of the American Frontier* [with the collaboration of J. B. Hedges], New York, 1949, p. 449.)

21. Allen George Lewes Shaw, *The Economic Development of Australia* (London, 1946), p. 11.

22. Lawson, *op. cit.,* Vol. I, pp. 33-34.

23. Billington, *op. cit.,* p. 11.

24. The term "West" is a comprehensive and loose one, and a good deal of difficulty can arise from this fact. However, to avoid a more detailed, but exceedingly cumbersome, description on every occasion, I have used it throughout, and mean by it the general area delineated here.

25. The United States Minister to Australia wrote in 1944: "As a boy I lived in the Cherokee strip when water was hauled from door to door and sold by the barrel. Some of my earliest recollections are concerned with conversations between men and women of that time about the drilling of wells and the character of the water tapped. I have heard all these problems discussed along this Australian grassland that I have just travelled . . . as in Oklahoma and Kansas . . ." (Charles Lydiard Aubrey Abbott, *Australia's Frontier Province,* Sydney, 1950, p. 210.)

26. Taylor, *op. cit.,* p. 62.

27. Quoted Walter Prescott Webb, *The Great Plains* (Boston, 1931), p. 422.

28. Having, within the space of nine months, driven with my

young family in two heat waves, first from Canberra to Brisbane and back through bush fires and a grasshopper invasion, and then from San Francisco to New York via Oklahoma City and Little Rock through the overhot winds of a summer drought, I can testify to these similarities from personal experience.

Notes to Chapter 2

1. My chief sources for these statistics are: *Historical Statistics of the United States 1789-1945* (Washington, 1949), and *Official Year Book of the Commonwealth of Australia,* No. 39, 1953 (Canberra, 1952).
2. Hancock, *Australia,* p. 53.
3. Eris O'Brien, *The Foundation of Australia, 1786-1800. A Study in English Criminal Practice and Penal Colonization in the Eighteenth Century* (London, 1937).
4. Miles Franklin and E. Dympha Cusack, *Pioneers on Parade* (Sydney 1939), p. 69.
5. As specimens of the Romantic novel it is interesting to compare Marcus Clarke's *For the Term of His Natural Life* with Harriet Beecher Stowe's *Uncle Tom's Cabin.*
6. Brent of Bin Bin, *op. cit.,* p. 19.
7. And also to show that the felons were in fact good men who were the victims of a cold-blooded and unjust social system in the mother-country, which seems somewhat more doubtful. Certainly as Russel Ward puts it, one can hardly justify the Australian conviction that "The transports were loaded to the gunwales . . . with Scottish Martyrs, Tolpuddle Martyrs, Irish democratic rebels (who were also martyrs) . . ." "Felons and Folksongs," article read in manuscript. See also Russel Ward, *The Australian Legend* (Melbourne, 1958), particularly Chapter II on "The Founding Fathers."
8. Hancock, *Australia,* p. 41.
9. The over-all rate of increase of the Australian population has steadily exceeded that of the United States ever since 1906, except in the years of World War II. But between 1901, when the Australian population numbered nearly four million, and 1950 Australia received about 1,400,000 immigrants; while between 1776, when the American population also numbered approximately four million, and 1945 the United States absorbed around 38,750,000 immigrants. The highest quinquennium of Australian immigration before World War II was 1921-25, when the average annual intake was 36,653, or

about .7% of the total population, but in 1950 there were 152,505 immigrants, or 1.8% of the population. The largest early year of American immigration was 1854, when she absorbed 427,833 immigrants, or 1.6% of her total population, but 1907 was the biggest year of all, when she swallowed the Gargantuan total of 1,285,349 newcomers, who, however, only constituted 1.5% of the U.S. population. These figures are not exactly comparable, since they are rectified differently for departures, but they are probably precise enough for our purpose. They are based on *Historical Statistics of the United States 1789-1945* and the *Official Year Book of the Commonwealth of Australia,* No. 39, 1953.

10. 490,000 were British, 105,000 Italian, 70,000 Dutch, 70,000 Polish, and 40,000 German; 225,000 were from eight other countries. (*The English-Speaking World,* January, 1956.)

11. As far as America is concerned, I have argued this somewhat contentious case in detail in *Great Britain and the United States,* pp. 98-108; it needs no proving for Australia. It should, however, be noted that the very large Irish element played an analogous part in both countries; this extends to concrete similarities, such as, for example, their role in city and state politics.

12. This stage in the development of the American frontier, the temporary "Indianization" of the pioneer, hardly existed in Australia. The occasional runaway convict could eke out an existence with the aborigines, but the drop in standards was too great for Western civilization to acquire much of value from the native way of life.

13. Stephen Vincent Benét, *Western Star* (London, 1944), p. 50.

14. Hancock, *Australia,* p. 33.

15. As Fred Alexander points out, there is an obvious parallel between the policy underlying the Proclamation of 1763 and the equally useless efforts of the Governers of New South Wales to confine the pastoralists within the "Nineteen Counties" in the second quarter of the nineteenth century. See p. 56.

16. Archibald Grenfell Price, *White Settlers and Native Peoples; An Historical Study of Racial Contacts Between English-Speaking Whites and Aboriginal Peoples in the United States, Canada, Australia and New Zealand* (Melbourne, 1950).

17. The hanging of seven men in 1838, for the massacre of twenty-eight natives at Myall Creek as a reprisal, must be counted to the Australian authorities for virtue.

18. The Minister for Territories (1956) is himself an expert on native affairs.

Notes to Chapter 3

1. Political geographers use the terms boundary, which is a line, and frontier, which is a zone, to express the difference.
2. Hancock, *Survey of British Commonwealth Affairs,* Vol. II, pp. 2-3. In his notes for discussion of "The Frontier: An American Hypothesis in British Imperial History" at the Tenth International Congress of Historical Sciences, Sir Keith Hancock makes what seems, at first sight, to be some reservations about this view. He points out that the frontiersmen of the American school were "nation-builders, not getters and spenders," and it is true that the emphasis of the Turner school has been in many senses political. But it would be wrong to suppose that the political phenomena of the frontier were not deeply and ineradicably rooted in economic life, and that Turner himself was not well aware of the fact. The analysis of the different frontiers in terms of different types of economic activity may be, in Hancock's word, "superficial," but beneath these lies a profound appreciation of the importance of physiography and the availability of land in the economic, and therefore political, life of the American nation.
3. Benét, *op. cit.,* pp. 50-51.
4. On November 16, 1788, Major Ross wrote from 'Sydney Cove': ". . . in the whole world there is not a worse country than what we have yet seen of this; all that is contiguous to us is so very barren and forbidding that it may with truth be said—here nature is reversed, and if not so, she is nearly worn out . . ." (G.B. Barton, *History of New South Wales from the Records,* Sydney, 1889, Vol. I, p. 500.)
5. Marcus Clarke, *For the Term of His Natural Life* (London, 1952), p. x (First published in 1874).
6. In time, of course, the novelty wears off, and the visitor, like the Australian, can find the Bush attractive. The white native, indeed, has a feeling for his land as such, which is not so often apparent to the observer in the United States; there is an element in the Australian of that love of the countryside which is often held to be so characteristic of the Englishman. But this very real love does contain within it a taste for grudging denigration, a lingering savor of something approaching contempt. Thus, Clarke not unjustly continues: "But the dweller in the wilderness acknowledges the subtle charm of this fantastic land of monstrosities. He becomes familiar with the beauty of loneliness. Whispered to by the myriad tongues of the wilderness, he learns the language of the barren and

uncouth, and can read the hieroglyphs of haggard gum-trees, blown into odd shapes, distorted by fierce hot winds, or cramped with cold nights, when the Southern Cross freezes in a cloudless sky of icy blue. The phantasmagoria of that wild dreamland termed the Bush interprets itself, and the Poet of our desolation begins to comprehend why free Esau loved his heritage of desert sand better than all the bountiful richness of Egypt."

7. It is interesting to note that, in the very early years of inexperience, Indian corn did better in Australia than any other crop, but its cultivation has never developed on a scale at all comparable, even relatively, to its development in America.

8. Rum remains the characteristic Australian spiritous liquor, its original supremacy having been confirmed by the widespread production of sugar in Queensland.

9. Another—Brent of Bin Bin—called drunkenness "the bane of the Colonies."

10. Miles Franklin, *All That Swagger* (Sydney, 1949), p. 227.

11. *The Works of the Right Honourable Edmund Burke* (London, 1864), Vol. I, p. 466.

12. Greenwood (Ed.), *Australia,* p. 79.

13. Australia has some 500 species of timber, predominantly eucalypt, compared with some 700 in the United States and Canada; of these Australian species, at least three fifths are hardwoods. Thus, the Australian continent has to import almost all its softwood; the timber for the structural work of a new brick house in which we lived in Canberra was imported, but the hardwood floors were of beautiful red Jarrah, or *Eucalyptus marginata.*

14. From our house in the Australian Capital Territory, we looked out upon the scattered and gnarled, and sometimes stunted, gum trees, which were the natural product of the Australian Bush; a month later, by a strange coincidence, our house in northern California looked out upon a grove of similar eucalypts, exotics imported (as many were) in the nineteenth century, but growing straight and strong and to great stature. There are, of course, areas of Australia also which produce superb specimens of the eucalypt.

15. Edward Shann, *An Economic History of Australia* (Cambridge, 1938), p. 236.

16. *Ibid.,* p. 247.

17. *Ibid.,* pp. 234-35.

18. At first they went via China to pick up cargoes of tea.

19. Taylor, *op. cit.,* p. 306.

20. Shann, *op. cit.,* p. 81.

NOTES

21. There was poetic justice in this splendid abundance of sheep, bearing fine-quality wool, developed largely from Macarthur's own flocks; he might well remember the angry words of Governor Bligh, whom he had helped to overthrow: "What have I to do with your sheep, Sir? Are you to have such flocks of sheep as no man ever heard of before? No, Sir!" (Shann, *op. cit.,* p. 43.

22. Billington, *op. cit.,* p. 687. The cattlemen's resentment of the sheepherders' invasion of their lands finds a faint echo in the historians of the frontier themselves (and indeed of the reading public), for they talk denigratingly of these "unromantic individuals" with their "bleating 'woolies'" *(Ibid.);* this is natural enough as an attitude toward those who were, in part, agents of the almost inevitable destruction of the romantic way of life of the cowboy. Nor is it lacking in a certain symbolism of the difference between the ethos of the two frontiers, for, however hard men tried, it did not prove possible to make out of the Australian stockman a real rival in romance to the cowboy.

23. Shann, *op. cit.,* p. 86.

24. *Ibid.,* p. 116.

25. Brian Fitzpatrick, *The British Empire in Australia: An Economic History 1834-1939* (Melbourne, 1941).

26. *Ibid.,* p. 193.

27. Between 1825 and 1850 they constituted approximately 20 percent of her total exports.

28. Allen, *op. cit.,* Chapter Three.

29. Adam Smith, *The Wealth of Nations* (London, 1910), Vol. I, p. 389.

30. Quoted Hancock, *Australia,* p. 14.

31. Quoted Gordon Greenwood (Ed.), *Australia: A Social and Political History* (Sydney, 1955), p. 55.

32. They built, for instance, dwellings which they considered suitable not merely to their climate but to their place in society. The station of the rich pastoralist, with its wide verandas, is the analogue of the porticoed colonial mansion of the planter, however different their appearance may be except in what they derive from their adaptation to their inhabitants' need for cool shade.

33. S. V. Benét, *John Brown's Body* (New York, 1927), p. 334.

34. Crawford, *op. cit.,* p. 109.

35. Benét, *John Brown's Body,* p. 334.

36. Abbott, *op. cit.,* p. 190.

37. Under an intelligent and energetic administration (1956), the Territory is really on the move at last. Nor is the drive con-

fined to the government; I spent one day motoring and talking with a large leaseholder in the Northern Territory, who had returned to the land after an enterprising career building up the highly efficient air service of central Australia. He bristled with technological ingenuity and enterprising plans, including the air conditioning of his men's new homes, an unheard of thing in most of Australia, let alone the Bush. I was very surprised when he told me that he had never been outside Australia, so much did he remind me of America.

38. When in Alice Springs the rum was passed around with coffee each morning at breakfast, I felt that I had really found the living frontier!

39. I spent, for instance, an exciting afternoon near Alice Springs watching stockmen "cutting out" steers from a herd.

Notes to Chapter 4

1. "Good soils have been the most continuous attraction to the farmer's frontier." (Frederick Jackson Turner, *The Frontier in American History,* New York, 1947 [first published in 1920], p. 18.)

2. Quoted Greenwood (Ed.), *Australia,* p. 78.

3. He quotes two famous sentences, one from each. "Plenty of good land, and liberty to manage their own affairs their own way, seem to be the two great causes of the prosperity of all new colonies." *(Wealth of Nations,* Vol. II, p. 69.) "The existence of an area of free land, its continuous recession, and the advance of American settlement westward, explain American development." (Turner, *op. cit.,* p. 1.) This, of course, has echoes in every agricultural society: we are often reduced, after all, to describing feudalism primarily as a system of land tenure.

4. This point is made by George Wilson Pierson in an article on "The Frontier and American Institutions: A Criticism of the Turner Theory," in the *New England Quarterly,* 15 (June, 1942).

5. Turner, *op. cit.,* p. 3.

6. The last state actually ceded its lands to the federal government in 1802. (The later case of Texas was, of course, an exception to the rule.)

7. Quoted Greenwood (Ed.), *Australia,* p. 78.

8. See Roy M. Robbins, *Our Landed Heritage; The Public Domain 1776-1936* (Princeton, 1942), for this and other aspects of American land legislation.

9. They were most influential of all in the development of New Zealand, though they had some influence in Canada.

10. The measure, however, offered land very much cheaper—as well as being more liberal and democratic—than anything which existed in the Old World.

11. There were also Acts in 1832, 1834, 1838, and 1841, those of 1832 and 1834 being renewals of an Act of 1830.

12. Billington, *op. cit.,* p. 701.

13. See Stephen H. Roberts, *History of Australian Land Settlement (1788-1920)* (Melbourne, 1924).

14. This was almost exactly the same as the $1.25 an acre at which the minimum price of American land stood between 1820 and 1862.

15. No credit was therefore allowed.

16. Fitzpatrick, *op. cit.,* p. 146. See Appendix 7 of this work for further details of Australian land legislation.

17. Squatters "outside" were required to take out grazing licenses at £10 per annum, which gave them a kind of back-handed recognition, in the hope that authorization of occupation might enable some sort of check to be kept on them.

18. Fitzpatrick, *op. cit.,* p. 147.

19. Greenwood (Ed.), *Australia,* p. 104.

20. Shann, *op. cit.,* p. 199.

21. Greenwood (Ed.), *Australia,* p. 119.

22. *Ibid.,* p. 116.

23. Shann, *op. cit.,* p. 192.

24. Some squatters obtained "the perfect security of freehold" (Shann, *op. cit.,* p. 208), but in 1950, of a total area of 1,903,732,000 acres of Australian land, 55 percent (1,050,-956,000 acres) consisted of Crown lands on lease or license, though a high proportion of these were perpetual leases, which are not easy to distinguish from freehold *(Year Book,* 1953, p. 132). But the existence of leasehold in Australia constitutes an important distinction from American land laws, although it is interesting to note that President Hayes suggested a system of leasehold tenure for the cattle country of the West in 1877, a suggestion which came to nothing. Even under Theodore Roosevelt's conservation program and Franklin D. Roosevelt's continuation of it, only very tentative steps were taken in this direction, so that the leasing of government land remains much less usual than in Australia.

25. Fifty acres were granted to every person transporting a servant to Virginia in an effort to improve the supply of labor.

26. These were perhaps more pronounced in America than in Australia as was the part played in frontier development by

land companies, such as the Ohio Company and the Connecticut Land Company, despite the importance of the Australian Agricultural Company and the Van Diemen's Land Company.

27. Canada, like the United States, was at first (after the fur-trading dominion had waned) predominantly a land of small pioneer farmers, and to this day retains something of this character on the Prairies. Freehold, not leasehold, was her characteristic tenure.

28. Adam Smith had already noticed the importance of this wide distribution of American land in 1776.

29. Quoted S. E. Morison and H. S. Commager, *Growth of the American Republic,* Vol. II (London, 1942), p. 198.

30. "Banjo" Paterson, quoted Shann, *op. cit.,* p. 108.

31. Robbins, *op. cit.,* p. 49.

32. *The Cambridge History of the British Empire,* Vol. III, Part I: *Australia* (Cambridge, 1933), p. 194.

33. Squatter sovereignty in the United States had an ultra-democratic air; squatter sovereignty in Australia could only have been oligarchical.

Notes to Chapter 5

1. For the history of previous gold mining in the United States, see W.P. Morrell, *Gold Rushes* (London, 1940), which also treats of the whole international history of modern gold mining.

2. Greenwood (Ed.), *Australia,* p. 99. There were occasionally signs of the same spirit in America; J.A. Sutter, on whose land gold was first found in California, was, not without reason as it transpired, fearful of the consequences; and on a number of occasions military commanders in the West are said to have concealed the knowledge of local gold discoveries from their men lest they desert. But the view did not prevail for a quarter of a century and more among those holding political power, as it did in Australia.

3. Crawford, *op. cit.,* pp. 117-18. For consideration of the extent to which lawlessness actually prevailed on the gold fields in America, see note 15 below.

4. Silver, because of its lower value, required more capital and more organization at an earlier stage than gold; Broken Hill and the Comstock Lode are the embodiments of this fact. The same is true *a fortiori,* of uranium, which requires highly complex processing from the very beginning, though in the search

even for radioactive ores the only addition to the simple equipment needed by the prospector is a Geiger counter.

5. A prospector born in 1830 in America might reasonably have spent a lifetime in the search for gold, and have seen the opening up of the fields in California, Eastern Australia, the remaining West of the United States, South Africa, and Western Australia. His twentieth century successors fell on leaner years, but they exist nonetheless; Russel Ward records: "On the train to Alice Springs in January 1939, I met a prospector who had been 'making wages' on a creek in the Australian Alps. He was hurrying to a new 'strike,' of which he had heard, at Moonlight Rock-hole, thirty-six miles west of Tennant's Creek." *(Historical Studies; Australia and New Zealand,* May, 1955, p. 469 note 44.) The coming of atomic power has for a brief period restored the glory of the individual prospector in both America and Australia; the rich Australian uranium deposits at Rum Jungle in the Northern Territory were discovered by men who borrowed a Geiger counter for an afternoon's fun in the Bush.

6. Fitzpatrick, *op. cit.,* Chapter III.

7. Yet there were some reverse effects. The "Sydney cove," or "Sydney duck," figures in the lore of the American mining frontier. Laramie, for some reason, boasted of a newspaper called the *Boomerang,* and Russel Ward has discovered Australian Bush ballads which were well-known in the United States. (The Vigilantes of San Francisco took steps to exclude bad Australian elements in the early days. See Alan Valentine, *Vigilante Justice,* New York, 1956.) The "Australian ballot" was, no doubt, largely a nominal influence, but the South Australian system of land registry was apparently more than that (Roberts, *op. cit.,* p. 220). The ultimate effect, even if indirect, of Australian moves in the direction of social welfare has probably been substantial.

8. Fitzpatrick, *op. cit.,* p. 186.

9. Shann, *op. cit.,* p. 172.

10. Charles Howard Shinn, *Mining Camps; A Study in American Frontier Government* (New York, 1948), pp. 266-67; first published in 1885.

11. Frederic L. Paxson, *History of the American Frontier 1763-1893* (Cambridge, Mass., 1924), p. 373.

12. This is a difficult subject, upon which much interesting work might be done, particularly on the Australian side. Thus Shinn *(op. cit.,* p. 279) noted the importance of the American influence on the Australian fields, stating that the many Californians left "a strong impress upon the local mining legislation

and 'miners' councils' of Australia, particularly of Victoria," but one suspects that he was reading his American experience into that of Australia, and hence to some extent misunderstanding the nature and importance of the effects. (See Morrell, *op. cit.*, pp. 256-57.)

13. Yet in Australian myth the legend of Eureka loomed very large—until the historians, after their fashion, administered a douche of cold realism to this popular warm-spring of Australian democracy.

14. T.A. Rickard, *A History of American Mining* (New York, 1932).

15. This reputation was to some, perhaps to a considerable, extent undeserved. See, for instance, Shinn, *op. cit.*, and, for another district than California, Thomas M. Marshall, "The Miners' Laws of Colorado," in the *American Historical Review,* April, 1920.

16. Thomas A. Browne, *Robbery Under Arms* (London, 1937), p. 259. First published in 1888.

17. Nevertheless, there is an analogy here with the fact that pressure from California itself was crucial in forcing Congress to grant it statehood.

18. The Australian figure for 1850 was 405,356; the estimates of American population for 1630 and 1640 are 5,700 and 26,947.

19. There would appear, however, to be a lineal descent of ideas from frontier inflationism at this time to twentieth century Social Credit doctrines, which have had their greatest strength in the western provinces of Canada.

Notes to Chapter 6

1. Bowman, *op. cit.*, p. 48. Even the American miners, who made, as Morrell points out *(op. cit.*, p. 193) remarkable technical advances, had to rely on the scientific geologist "from the wider civilization of which it [California] formed a part."

2. Semple, *op. cit.*, p. 254.

3. This can still be clearly seen in the scarcity of north-south lines west of the Mississippi compared with the number of those which run from east to west.

4. The lack of a unifying westward movement was also partly responsible for the fact that Australia has always had three different major railway gauges. In 1945 the United States had about 400,000 miles of railroad track, Australia had somewhat over 30,000 miles.

5. On the roadside some miles outside Alice Springs there stands

a small and simple monolith, raised to the memory of "Flynn of the Inland," who was the pioneer of this venture.

6. Franklin, *op. cit.,* p. 99.
7. Katharine S. Prichard, *Working Bullocks* (London, 1944), p. 79.
8. In Australia they came complete with Afghan drivers, which is still commemorated in the odd fact that the trains from Adelaide to Alice Springs are known as the "Ghans," the better of the two being described as the "Flash Ghan." The Oriental aspect of the Western United States was short-lived, for the camels died out. But there is a chance that it may endure in Australia, for swinging round a corner on a Bush track in the Northern Territory, our car came suddenly upon a frightened family of three camels, now quite wild but acclimatized to life in the Bush.
9. Billington, *op. cit.,* p. 638.
10. I spent an interesting hour on a station many miles from Alice Springs listening to a doctor giving medical advice over the radio about the treatment of a patient whose symptoms were described to him by the same medium; radio can also serve much more mundane purposes, such as ordering urgent supplies, or even relieving loneliness by a little talk.
11. "Rustlers" in America, "duffers" in Australia.
12. Ridley's stripper became known in America, and later in the century American combine harvesters were shipped to Australia.
13. See Chapter VII, note 98 below.
14. One of the chief instruments making desert living possible has been air conditioning, the development of which in the last decade is in the most energetic American tradition of making, and then making economical, remarkable technical improvements. Its spread was the single most striking change to the eye of at least one visitor in 1954, who had not been in America since 1949.

Notes to Chapter 7

1. Turner, *op. cit.,* pp. 3-4.
2. See S. J. Baker, *The Australian Language* (Sydney, 1945), and H. L. Mencken, *The American Language* (New York, 1946).
3. No one present in Australia during the Royal Tour of 1953-54 could have any doubts on this point; neither distance nor flood nor fire was able to prevent most Australians from get-

ting at least a glimpse of the first reigning monarch ever to visit Australia.

4. For this idea I am indebted to my friend Professor R. M. Hartwell.

5. Crawford, *op. cit.*, p. 149. This is still true of Australian literature; as Russel Ward points out, in a 1953 literary anthology, *Australia Writes* (edited by T. Inglis Moore), "Twenty-four of the twenty-nine prose contributions exhibit more or less strong 'outback' influence in spirit, in setting, or in both." *(Historical Studies: Australia and New Zealand,* May, 1955, p. 470 note.)

6. Tom Collins (Joseph Furphy), *Such Is Life; Being Certain Extracts from the Diary of Tom Collins* (London, 1948), pp. 80-81.

7. Turner, *op. cit.*, p. 261.

8. *Ibid.*, p. 345.

9. Quoted Allen, *op. cit.*, p. 149.

10. Hancock *Australia,* p. 54.

11. This is a relevant excerpt:

> Give me your tired, your poor,
> Your huddled masses yearning to breathe free,
> The wretched refuse of your teeming shore,
> Send these, the homeless, tempest-tossed to me:
> I lift my lamp beside the golden door.

12. Xavier Herbert, *Capricornia* (Sydney, 1947), pp. 320-21.

13. Greenwood (Ed.), *Australia,* p. 206.

14. *Ibid.*, p. 199.

15. Crawford, *op. cit.*, p. 66.

16. Clarke, *op. cit.*, p. x.

17. See pp. 28-9 above.

18. *Prose Works,* Vol. I, p. 192.

19. *Ibid.*, p. 54. The English inheritance seems to show itself in the understatement of Australian humor; as Collins *(op. cit.,* p. 207) wrote of Bush life: "No young fellow . . . dared to embellish his narrative in the slightest degree, on pain of being posted as a double-adjective blatherskite . . ." American frontier humor, on the other hand, was of a directly contrary order: "They were insufferable braggarts, the Mississippi Valley frontiermen . . . 'I'm the darling branch of old Kentuck that can eat a painter, hold a buffalo out to drink and put a rifle-ball through the moon,' one would shout," and be answered in like vein. (Billington, *op. cit.*, p. 481.)

20. *Ibid.*, p. 278.

21. Bundle traditionally carried by all bushmen.

22. *Prose works,* Vol. II, pp. 189-90.
23. Quoted Webb, *op. cit.,* p. 470.
24. *Prose Works,* Vol. II, p. 184.
25. Quoted Webb, *op. cit.,* pp. 472-73. Webb even points out that there is no place in the West, unlike the Mississippi Valley apparently, for "loquaciousness, for braggadocio, for exhibition of a superlative ego . . . There is . . . fun of an indirect nature" (*op. cit.,* p. 247). This produces a humor of understatement very like that of Australia.
26. If only because it had great publicity value.
27. Turner, *op. cit.,* pp. 298-99.
28. For the full version of his lament, see pp. 11-12, above.
29. Hancock, *Australia,* pp. 57-58.
30. Turner, *op. cit.,* p. 30.
31. *Ibid.,* p. 4.
32. *Ibid.,* p. 65.
33. Notably Benjamin F. Wright, as for instance in Dixon Ryan Fox (Ed.), *Sources of Culture in the Middle West* (New York, 1934).
34. We may compare the words of William Westgarth: "The independent bearing of the colonial labouring population . . . is often commented upon. A labourer in Australia is indeed a very different personage from one in the mother country, and he is not long of knowing the fact" (Crawford, *op cit.,* p. 124), with those of Crèvecoeur: "A European, when he first arrives, seems limited in his intentions, as well as in his views: but he very suddenly alters his scale . . .; he now feels himself a man, because he is treated as such; . . . this first swell inspires him with those new thoughts which constitute an American . . ." (Allen, *op. cit.,* p. 219).
35. *Prose Works,* Vol. II, p. 391. This particular manifestation of Australian disregard, if not contemptuous defiance, of the law is still visible today; only when the reservoirs in Canberra were actually on the point of running dry did its inhabitants in 1954 cease the forbidden use in droughty times of their garden hoses. See p. 104, below.
36. Hancock, *Australia,* p. 270.
37. Collins, *op. cit.,* p. 205.
38. *Ibid.,* p. 81. This reads a trifle oddly after World War II.
39. Turner, *op. cit.,* p. 240.
40. *Ibid.,* p. 270.
41. *Ibid.,* p. 259.
42. His exchanges with President Wilson at the Peace Conference of 1919 had all this frontier brashness, and grated accordingly—as they were intended to do—on the ears and sensibilities of the one-time Princeton professor.

43. Hancock, *Australia,* p. 271.
44. I have studied the history of nineteenth century Anglo-American relations too much to be willing to follow in the footsteps of British travelers in America by making supercilious and offensive comments about Australian manners, but Australians take a positive pride in their toughness, and on occasion this shows itself in a contempt for hygiene. On our first picnic in the Bush our Australian host took the water for our "billy" from a billabong, which showed to a marked extent the propensity to "cream and mantle like a standing pond," with the airy remark that it would be all right when boiled! On the frontier proper, in the Northern Territory, another of my hosts handed me a dose of billy-tea in an old laboratory beaker, with the words, "I was afraid it might be stained with chemicals, but I'm still alive after two days' consumption!"
45. Turner, *op. cit.,* p. 211.
46. Henry Handel Richardson's great trilogy, *The Fortunes of Richard Mahoney* (Holt, 1917), may not only be held to bear comparison with the works of Henry James, but deals fascinatingly with the same theme of the expatriates, which is so prominent in *The American, Roderick Hudson,* and others. Both writers spent much of their lives, and ended their days in Britain.
47. Greenwood (Ed.), *Australia,* p. 236.
48. *Ibid.,* p. 234.
49. Crawford notes that in Western Australia, one of the frontier states, the eastern visitor still observes that neighborliness, which is also still detectable by the traveler west of the Mississippi.
50. *Prose Works,* Vol. II, p. 181.
51. The continuance and even degree of her leadership in some aspects of this field must not be exaggerated, for, according to Crawford, Australia in 1939 spent less per head of the population on social services than Great Britain.
52. Quoted Hancock, *Australia,* p. 57.
53. Turner, *op. cit.,* p. 270.
54. The importance of class in Australia does seem to imply that the relative classlessness of American nineteenth century political and social ideas may have something to do with America's peculiar frontier as Turner suggested, despite the misgivings of Louis M. Hacker (*The Nation,* 137, July 26, 1933).
55. *Prose Works,* Vol. I, p. 280.
56. *Ibid.,* p. 16.
57. See Appendix A.

58. Herbert, *op. cit.*, p. 330.
59. American rural unions were almost always dominated by the farmers. Thus of the Farmers' and Laborers' Union of America, which originated in Texas in the middle seventies, an historian writes at the time of a convention held in St. Louis in 1889 (when it numbered a million members): "This list of demands speaks volumes for the mental subjection of the Knights of Labor to the farmers' movement. None of these demands may be called a strictly labour demand . . ." (John R. Commons, *et al., History of Labour in the United States,* New York, 1918, p. 492). Even an extreme radical such as Thomas Skidmore, leader of the Agrarian Workingmen's Party of the 1830's, demanded the equalization of property for the individual members of society and had no notion of collectivism, while the more moderate agrarianism of the forties and fifties merely desired the distribution of the public lands in equal farm lots of 160 acres. This was the natural result of the predominance on the American frontier of the small farmer. By the time conditions had changed, the individualist tradition was deeply ingrained, which was one reason for the weakness and relatively rapid disappearance of the I.W.W., which made a serious effort in the early twentieth century to organize, among others, the migratory rural workers, particularly in the West.
60. For a full and interesting treatment of this fascinating topic, see Russel Ward, "Collectivist Notions of a Nomad Tribe," in *Historical Studies: Australia and New Zealand,* May, 1955, from which I quote in the ensuing paragraph (pp. 460, 468, 473).
61. See Appendix B for a good specimen of a Bush ballad.
62. Though it is not of anything like the same significance in the country as in the city, the constant mass immigration of cheap labor into the United States may have had some effect in checking rural unionization, as it certainly did the organization of urban labor.
63. Turner, *op. cit.*, p. 219.
64. *Ibid.*, p. 258.
65. Turner's advocacy of the safety valve theory was, as its most mordant and destructive critic points out, only "incidental" and "tacit" (Fred A. Shannon, "A Post Mortem on the Labor-Safety-Valve Theory," *Agricultural History,* 19, January, 1945, pp. 31-37), and indeed he is only credited (or debited) with two notable references to it by that critic. It is his disciples who have subsequently overstated it, though he gave it a kind of vague blessing.
66. For an interesting elucidation of this fact and its influence,

particularly in the Old Northwest, see Stanley Elkins and Eric McKitrick, "A Meaning for Turner's Frontier," in the *Political Science Quarterly*, 1954, p. 321 *et seq.* and p. 565 *et seq.* The second part of the article also provides much food for thought about the comparison between American planters and Australian squatters, and the way in which the former succeeded in maintaining their political as well as their economic power, which the latter, as we have seen, failed to do.

67. " 'The big man's frontier'—the squatter's priority—is probably the chief factor in any explanation of the major part played by the State in developmental work in Australia as compared with, for example, the United States of America." (Fitzpatrick, *op. cit.*, p. 191).

68. Two remarks illuminate these two aspects of Australian life. "Well, he came to my station on the Lachlan years ago without a penny in his pocket, . . . and I gave him a job. He's my boss now. Ah, well! it's the way of Australia . . ." (*Prose Works,* Vol. II, p. 133). "Lacking generations of development, there is no typical squatter." (Collins, *op. cit.*, p. 205).

69. Hancock writes (*Australia,* p. 181) that "the dominant passion of Australian labour is for substantial equality," and labor has set the tone for Australian life for the last half century and more. Indeed, one of the more interesting problems in Australian history is why the Australian scene has been dominated by the ideas of labor, although Labour governments in Canberra have really not predominated to this extent. Capitalist and socially conservative forces have received scant justice, even from Australian historians, for their vital part in the development of the continent.

70. Greenwood (Ed.), *Australia,* p. 205.

71. Hancock, *Australia,* p. 183.

72. *Prose Works,* Vol. II, p. 429.

73. *Prose Works,* Vol. I, p. 40.

74. Franklin, *op. cit.*, p. 99.

75. Turner, *op. cit.,* pp. 259-60.

76. Thus, the generalized, the perhaps deliberately imprecise, words of Turner (*op. cit.,* p. 275) still contain a considerable element of exact truth: ". . . the sanative influences of the free spaces of the West were destined to ameliorate labor's condition, to afford new hopes and new faith to pioneer democracy . . ." The stress is on aspiration rather than actuality, on the climate of living of the West rather than on the land itself.

77. As S. H. Roberts wrote of sheepherding, it was a "sordid, filthy existence, despite all the eulogies of free life in contact

with nature and communion with the gums. The only real contact was with a few degraded convicts and the eternal smell of sheep effluvia. Its sole return was monetary; in itself it was penal servitude of the worst type—there is no romance in monotony and mutton fat." (Quoted A. G. L. Shaw, *Story of Australia,* London, 1955, pp. 78-79.)

78. Turner, *op. cit.*, p. 212.
79. Billington, *op. cit.*, p. 58.
80. Not only does the initial disparity in population make a huge disproportion, but in addition the fact that so high a percentage of Australians live in great cities makes the rural dispersion wider yet; it is still wide even if we discount the virtually unoccupied dead heart. In 1949 the United States had a population density of 49.4 persons per square mile and Australia of 2.7, the lowest of any great country in the world. The conclusion must not be drawn from this, however, that Australia is ever very likely to be able to support a population comparable in size with that of the United States.
81. Turner, *op. cit.*, p. 212 and pp. 32-33 note.
82. "Lynch law was a characteristic rather of American frontier societies than of frontiers in general . . ." (Leyburn, *op. cit.*, p. 219). Leyburn points out that the only parallel to the Vigilantes was the Boer Commandos; the Texas Rangers were originally volunteers, but were then officially recognized and came very much to resemble the Australian troopers. The Canadian Northwest Mounted Police were an even more effective force than the Australian in the control of the frontier. On California's reputation for lawlessness, see p. 64 above.
83. Hancock, *Australia*, p. 39.
84. Crawford, *op. cit.*, p. 118.
85. Quoted Webb, *op. cit.*, p. 453.
86. Herbert, *op. cit.*, p. 480.
87. It is possible that the Irish strain is important here.
88. Food.
89. *Prose Works,* Vol. II, p. 314.
90. Turner, *op. cit.*, p. 29.
91. This feeling was undoubtedly encouraged by the frontier, despite the early nineteenth century willingness of parts of the Mississippi Valley to look to Spain when discontented with the federal government.
92. See Alexander, *op. cit.*, p. 30.
93. Turner, *op. cit.*, p. 294.
94. Franklin, *op. cit.*, p. 101.
95. Turner, *op. cit.*, p. 306.

96. Of California mining for example, Morrell (*op. cit.*, p. 193) wrote, ". . . none of the earlier gold rushes had anything like the same record of technical achievement."

97. The South would seem to be the main exception, but, for all its seeming inefficiencies, we must not underestimate its energetic and skillful achievement in dominating, as it did, the world's cotton markets.

98. In part, also, of course, it is due to the richness of America's resources, and, in part, without doubt, to the enlightened educational policy of the great republic, which always had a practical tendency. As the United States had done, Australia tried from the twenties on to establish education by a system of land grants, and there was great interest in the question in the early years of self-government, but from the beginning the matter was not well handled and was confused (as in Britain) by the issue of Church control. Its governments were not, in any case, ready so soon to subsidize technological education as the Americans.

99. Shann, *op. cit.*, p. 284. I heard many contemporary accounts of similar, though necessarily much more elaborate, repairs to cars which had broken down in the vastness of the outback.

100. Perhaps it is not unfair to say that it shows itself only in sport!

101. I am indebted for this and other ideas on the Australian frontier to my friend L. F. Fitzhardinge, Reader in the Sources of Australian History in the Australian National University.

102. *Prose Works,* Vol. I, p. 227.

103. *Ibid.*, p. 337.

104. As one acid-tongued Australian lady said to me: "Ours is a Mediterranean climate. We have not adopted the habit of the siesta. We content ourselves with taking a mental siesta all the time." She added later, "Yes, other peoples in warm climates are dirty and lazy but picturesque and colorful. Australians are just dirty and lazy."

105. Benét, *op. cit.*, p. 5.

106. Collins, *op. cit.*, p. 1.

Notes to Chapter 8

1. In the final paragraph of his original essay Turner (*op. cit.*, p. 38) showed the native openness of his mind by these words: "What the Mediterranean Sea was to the Greeks, breaking the bond of custom, offering new experiences, calling out new institutions and activities, that, and more, the ever retreating

frontier has been to the United States directly, and to the nations of Europe more remotely."

2. *Ibid.*, p. 11.
3. The frontier hypothesis is indeed a remarkable exemplification of Toynbee's thesis of challenge and response; it is *par excellence* the "stimulus of new ground" (Toynbee, *op. cit.*, p. 99). The American environment is the golden mean of challenge, whereas that of Australia is perhaps just a trifle too hard to produce quite as strong a response.
4. When once the South had lost its initial eighteenth century lead, the process of populating the West was, in military terms, a gigantic turning-movement of the North, pivoting roughly on the junction of the Ohio with the Mississippi.
5. Turner, *op. cit.*, p. 264.
6. *Ibid.*, p. 37.
7. Quoted Turner, *op. cit.*, p. 153.
8. Carl Lotus Becker, "Frederick Jackson Turner," in *American Master of Social Science: An Approach to the Study of the Social Sciences Through a Neglected Field of Biography,* Howard W. Odum (Ed.) (New York, 1927), p. 295.
9. See Allen, *op. cit., passim.*
10. Some of the liveliest of these were led, aptly enough, by an Australian rejoicing in the name of Frank Melbourne.

APPENDIX A

WALTZING MATILDA[1]

A. B. Paterson

Once a jolly swagman[2] camped by a billabong[3]
Under the shade of a coolibah[4] tree,
And he sang as he watched and waited till his billy[5] boiled,
"You'll come awaltzing Matilda[6] with me!"

Chorus Waltzing Matilda, Waltzing Matilda,
          You'll come awaltzing Matilda with me.
          And he sang as he watched and waited till his billy boiled.
          "You'll come awaltzing Matilda with me!"

Down came a jumbuck[7] to drink at the billabong,
Up jumped the swagman and grabbed him with glee,
And he sang as he stowed that jumbuck in his tucker[8] bag,
"You'll come awaltzing Matilda with me!"

Chorus Waltzing Matilda, Waltzing Matilda,
          You'll come awaltzing Matilda with me.
          And he sang as he stowed that jumbuck in his tucker bag.
          "You'll come awaltzing Matilda with me!"

Up rode the squatter,[9] mounted on his thoroughbred,
Down came the troopers, one, two, three:
"Where's that jolly jumbuck You've got in your tucker bag?"
"You'll come awaltzing Matilda with me!"

Chorus Waltzing Matilda, Waltzing Matilda,
          You'll come awaltzing Matilda with me.
          "Where's that jolly jumbuck You've got in your tucker
              bag?"
          "You'll come awaltzing Matilda with me!"

Up jumped the swagman, sprang into the billabong.
"You'll never catch me alive," said he.

APPENDIX A

And his ghost may be heard as you pass by that billabong,
"You'll come awaltzing Matilda with me!"

Chorus   Waltzing Matilda, Waltzing Matilda,
       You'll come awaltzing Matilda with me.
       And his ghost may be heard as you pass by that billabong,
       "You'll come awaltzing Matilda with me!"

[1] Copyright 1936 by Allen & Co., Pty., Ltd., Melbourne, Australia. Copyright 1941 by Carl Fischer, Inc., New York.

[2] A man on tramp carrying his swag, which means a bundle wrapped up in a blanket.

[3] A water hole in the dried-up bed of a river.

[4] Eucalyptus tree.

[5] A tin can used as a kettle.

[6] Waltzing Matilda, carrying one's bundle ("swag"), or going on the tramp.

[7] A sheep.

[8] Food.

[9] A sheep farmer on a large scale.

APPENDIX B

THE WALLABY BRIGADE

Anon.

You often have been told of regiments brave and bold,
But we are the bravest in the land;
We're called the Rag-Tag Band, and we rally in Queensland,
We are members of the Wallaby Brigade.

Chorus   Tramp, tramp, tramp across the borders,
          The swagmen are rolling up I see.
          When the shearing's at an end we'll go fishing in a bend.
          Then Hurrah! for the Wallaby Brigade.

When you are leaving camp, you must ask some brother tramp,
If there are any jobs to be had,
Or what sort of a shop that station is to stop,
For a member of the Wallaby Brigade.

You ask if they want men, you ask for rations then,
If they don't stump up a warning should be made;
To teach them better sense—Why, "Set fire to their fence,"
Is the war cry of the Wallaby Brigade.

The squatters thought us done when they fenced in all their run,
But a prettier mistake they never made;
You've only to sport your dover and knock a monkey over,[1]
There's cheap mutton for the Wallaby Brigade.

Now when the shearing's in our harvest will begin,
Our swags for a spell down will be laid;
But when our cheques are drank we will join the Rag-Tag rank,
Limeburners[2] in the Wallaby Brigade.

[1] "Monkey" is slang for sheep, and "to knock over" means to kill.
[2] Swagmen.
(Quoted Russel Ward, "Felons and Folksongs," article read in manuscript.)

Index

INDEX

146

INDEX

150

LUIS

Ugv
GF
51
A4